Pure Types are Rare

Pure Types are Rare

Myths and
Meanings of Madness

Irwin Silverman

PRAEGER

PRAEGER SPECIAL STUDIES • PRAEGER SCIENTIFIC

Library of Congress Cataloging in Publication Data

Silverman, Irwin.
  Pure types are rare.

  Includes bibliographical references and index.
  1. Mental illness.   2. Insanity.   I. Title.
RC454.4.S54   1983   362.2   82-22480
ISBN 0-03-063369-9

Published in 1983 by Praeger Publishers
CBS Educational and Professional Publishing
a Division of CBS Inc.
521 Fifth Avenue, New York, New York 10175 U.S.A.

3456789 052 987654321

Printed in the United States of America
on acid-free paper

To the memory of my mother
who taught me to pay more attention to
what people *do* than what they *say*

PREFACE

As a student trainee more than two decades ago, I happened on the psychiatric ward late one evening and found the *catatonic schizophrenic*, who had always maintained the mutism characteristic of his diagnosis in my presence, chatting amiably with another patient. "The catatonic speaks," I burst into my supervisor's office the next day with the news. "He just doesn't talk around us." "Pure types are rare," he shrugged. Subsequently, I discovered that pure, and even minimally respectable types, are rarer than rare. They are virtually nonexistent except in the minds and textbooks of professionals.

This book attempts to document and explain the mummery of the mental-health movement. It is about both madness and mental illness, and the dubious relationship between them. Madness is viewed as a mode of response to conflict or crisis; oblique, but explicable, as is all behavior, in terms of its adaptive functions for the individual. Mental illness is regarded as the core concept of an ideology, primarily employed in the covert exercise of social power. Victims of the mental-illness ideology include mad people, in the minority, but are mainly composed of "nuisance populations": those who impede some aim or stray from some norm of society. Consequently, the rhetoric of the mental-illness ideology obfuscates rather than facilitates the understanding of madness.

I have presented much of this material in lectures. Many in the audiences who did not regard the data and conclusions lightly nevertheless found it difficult to conceive that a respected profession, with the sanction of society, could be routinely engaged in oppression in the guise of humanitarian and scientific values. I reminded them of similar, painful revelations, in societies that also regarded themselves as sophisticated and civilized, concerning, for example, the vulnerability of women and heretics to demonic possession, the subhuman nature of black slaves, or the genetic inferiority of non-Aryan races. One of the enigmas of the human condition is our profound capacity for self-delusion, when it suits us. The movement of civilization has embodied a succession of ideologies that mask some program of intimidation and control by the socially powerful over the powerless; each rationalized, following its demise, as the machinations of an ill-informed or dispassionate age. One may hope for signs of more enlightened progress, but needs to be content to strive for interim triumphs of truth and justice.

For nearly two decades, Thomas Szasz was virtually the sole beacon in the darkness of the mental-health field; lately, he has been joined by some others. I exclude the "revisionists": those who discuss misdirections and abuses within the system rather than the unqualified misdirection and abuse of the total system. I regard them as I might have regarded revisionists within the witchcraft, slavery, or Nazi movements: perhaps well intentioned, but, on the whole, contributing to the propagation of the lie rather than its end. In the sections of this book dealing with the fallacies of the mental-health movement, I am beholden to Szasz. Where I am directly beholden, of course, I have cited him. Where I have not cited him, I am nevertheless beholden. His were the grand truths; we who follow can only try to fill gaps.

My attempts to reformulate madness were based largely on actual cases, although I have altered details of examples to render individuals unrecognizable. I owe a large debt to those who allowed and encouraged me to follow my heresies within the system, particularly Wally Coe, David Hackney, and Gary Stuart. Bob Baringer and my wife, Robin Alter, both shared with me for many hours the pains of truth-seeking and their ideas, in the process, surely became entangled with mine. I thank David Bakan for his salubrious comments on an earlier draft of the manuscript and Michael Bagby for his able research assistance.

Finally, I am grateful to the mad people, who guided me at least as much as I may have guided them.

FOREWORD
by Thomas Szasz

Like the relationship between parent and child, the relationship between various helpers and their beneficiaries is an integral part of the human condition. The agenda of the parent-child relationship is obvious: to protect the helpless infant and to nurture it until it is able to care for itself. However, the agendas of certain other helping relationships are often not so obvious.

Consider, for example, the relationship between exorciser and exorcised. The agenda of this relationship, in the Age of Faith, was exorcism—that is, helping the victim rid himself of the demons possessing him. Similar examples abound. Mesmer cured by manipulating "magnetic fluid," Mary Baker Eddy by combatting "Malicious Animal Magnetism," Freud by "redistributing libido," Reich by "accumulating orgones." Each of these agendas was identified by means of a key concept, the actual (material) existence of which either was obviously imaginary or fictitious, or soon proved to be so.

What would the agenda of the exorcist look like to a person living in the Middle Ages whose ideas about exorcism were like ours rather than like those of his contemporaries? What did the agenda of Mesmerism look like to someone who did not believe in "Mesmeric fluid"? What does the agenda of psychoanalysis look like to someone who does not believe in "libido"?

Modern psychiatry—indeed, the whole modern mental-health movement—has as its agenda the diagnosis and treatment of mental diseases. Mental illness is the key concept with which we now bestow meaning on the coming together of so-called mental patients and mental-health professionals. But suppose that the existence of mental illness is as fictitious as was the existence of demons, Mesmeric fluid, libido, or orgone?

Most psychiatrists, psychologists, and other mental-health professionals confidently assert that "mental illness exists" and is "like any other illness." Still, the fact remains that mental illness is not something a person can see or smell, taste or touch, hear or measure with an instrument. Since mental illness has no material existence, it is easy to see why, "scientific" protestations to the contrary notwithstanding, mental illness continues to be a mystifying idea or entity. Can we make it less so?

There are two ways of making mental illness less mystifying than it is. One way is by uncritically accepting the declarations of mental-health professionals about what mental illness is and what we should do about it. That is the way of the true believer.

The other way is by ignoring the term "mental illness" and focusing instead on what we can see and hear. In the mental-health field, what we can see and hear is what so-called mental patients, their families, and their professionally accredited helpers say and do. However, to be able to see and hear what these persons do and say requires a willingness to relinquish the customary ways of perceiving and describing mental illness and mental treatment. That is the way of the sceptic and of the true scientist. It is the way Professor Irwin Silverman has taken in pursuing the subject and presenting it to us.

Professor Silverman kindly credits me with having also done so, indeed with having led an exodus, as it were, out of an Egypt in which our vision of the human condition was enslaved by the false idols of health and illness. There has, however, been no exodus. The bondage in which the medical perspective is holding our view of human predicaments seems scarcely less secure now than it was when I first tried to break its grip a quarter of a century ago. The captivity in which the categories of "illness" and "treatment" hold the modern mind is, moreover, a metaphorical enslavement: after all, it is a self-enslavement. Accordingly, Professor Silverman's efforts to break these bonds, held fast by the shackles of language and law, habit and professional self-interest, have been necessary and well spent. Indeed, Professor Silverman has done more than cast off the shackles of the "medical model": by showing us how he has done so he helps the reader do the same for himself. Finally, by showing us what "mental healing" would be like without psychiatric pretentions and illusions, without the utter falseness of the modern mental-health industry, he points the way toward social policies based on common sense and decency rather than on paternalism and scientism.

In short, Professor Silverman has succeeded admirably in the task which he has set himself: he has produced a book about our perennial human problems and predicaments and our efforts to cope with them, and it is serious without being ponderous, honest without being maudlin, well written without being slick. It deserves a large and appreciative audience.

CONTENTS

PURE TYPES ARE RARE:
Mental Illness in the
Eye of the Beholder

A MOST UNREMARKABLE COLLECTION
OF HUMANKIND

In 1958, I gained the right to enter as a graduate student trainee into the psychiatric ward of a government hospital. Expecting to be thrust among the macabre mass of mental aberrants so dramatically depicted in my textbooks, I found, instead, a most unremarkable collection of humankind. True, they could not, as a group, be regarded as pillars of their communities. There were boozers and brawlers, derelicts and deviants, malcontents and misfits of every variety. Some were very angry, some very sad, and some, though not many, sometimes behaved rather peculiarly, meaning incomprehensibly to me. Nevertheless, they bore little resemblance to their exotic clinical descriptions. Their tales were not of sudden or progressive mental derangement, but of hard times and frustration, jobs lost, lovers fled, aspirations modest and grand, unfulfilled and abandoned. Their attitudes and demeanors appeared not as products of diseased brains, but as explicable expressions of powerlessness, futility, and despair. They were not unlike many you might encounter on the wrong side of the tracks, and inasmuch as I have observed that very few mental-health professionals linger in the seamy corners of society before taking the narrow paths to their degrees and titles, they may have been seen as much more atypical than they really were.

But the revelation that people inside mental hospitals are

medically indistinguishable from those outside does not come easily to the casual observer or the student. The diagnostic labels are intimidating – for example, *manic depressive psychosis, catatonic schizophrenia, involutional melancholia* – and neither layman nor neophyte will readily reject the gospel of white-coated eminences with M.D.'s or Ph.D.'s. The student has the additional burden of a heavy, personal stake in a newly launched career as a mental illness expert and may find it difficult to tolerate the notion that there may not be such a thing. He reasons, instead, that the manifestations of serious mental disorder are probably too subtle to be detected by the untrained eye and ear.

THE ART OF PSYCHODIAGNOSIS

So, humble and eager, I proceeded to study the fine art of psychodiagnosis, about which the *Comprehensive Textbook of Psychiatry*, one of the most authoritative sources in the field, says: "Psychiatric classification is in many ways a deceptively simple matter. . . . It is surprising how quickly the average resident in training can learn to comply with the formal requirements." [1]

Simple? Yes. Three maverick professors, in fact, gave 19 college freshmen a "crash course" in psychiatry, using a programmed instructional method, followed by the psychiatric section of the National Board Examinations, which are designed for graduating M.D.'s. Their average study time was 12.3 hours; their average score was an acceptable 61 percent.[2]

Deceptively simple? Not really. In most cases psychiatric diagnoses are made on the basis of one brief interview. Scheff found the average time for court-ordered assessments to be 9.2 minutes,[3] though that may not be typical. I suspect a truer overall average would be between thirty and forty minutes. How does a psychiatrist reach a conclusion in 9.2 or thirty or forty minutes? He simply focusses on some characteristic or recent behavior of the person and translates this into its clinical name. Thus, if the person tends to blame others for his woes, he is a *paranoid*; if he blames himself, a *depressive*, and if he doesn't seem to care enough to blame anything, *schizoid*. If he drinks, call him an *alcoholic*; if he beats his wife, an *explosive personality*; if he has run afoul of the law, a *sociopath*.

I recall a silent, scowling, middle-aged patient of my student years, who spent most of the day in the same armchair in a corner of the dayroom within view of the television set and who communicated mainly by gestures and grunts. He was called *catatonic schizophrenic*, and though the immobility and mutism that characterizes this disorder was certainly not as blatant in this case as in my textbook illustrations, it sufficed for me, until I happened on the ward late one evening to find him chatting amiably with his roommate.

"The catatonic speaks," I said bursting into my supervisor's office the next morning. "He just doesn't talk around us."

"We know that." He grinned at me.

"Then he's not catatonic, is he?" I was truly puzzled.

"He's catatonic enough." He shrugged. "Pure types are rare. Besides, what else would we call him?"

I attended the staff rounds of another patient, a procedure similar to general medical rounds except that instead of physicians perusing bodies and charts at bedsides, the patient sits at one end of a conference table while the staff, led by the attending psychiatrist, questions him. This patient was an elderly man, obviously very unhappy. His psychiatrist astutely led him through all of his complaints about the hospital to his major "delusion": that his siblings, in complicity with his doctors, were engaged in a plot to keep him in the hospital so they could take complete control of the family business. When he was dismissed from the conference, everyone agreed with the diagnosis of *paranoid schizophrenia*.

I asked, with all of the deference I could muster, whether there might be some truth in his beliefs. I was told, offhandedly, that there was, in fact, a competency hearing in progress. He had been mishandling the business anyway, according to the family, and they would need total control while he was institutionalized in order to keep it going.

"Then can we call it a delusion?" I pressed.

The psychiatrist looked at me sharply. "Well, certainly there is no plot involving the hospital to take his business away." Then he asked pointedly, "Do you think there is?"

I was past the point of return, but I chose my words carefully.

"I might not call it a plot, but his family is responsible for him being here and losing control of his business, and we are cooperating with them. I can see where it may look like a plot from his perspective."

The psychiatrist merely smiled. "That is the point, of course. His *perspective* is paranoid." Everyone else nodded.

PSYCHIATRISTS AND PSEUDOPATIENTS

Maurice Temberlin reported a study in 1970 in which a recording of a staged, clinical interview was played to 100 practicing psychiatrists and psychologists.[4] Half of them were told that the subject of the interview was a hospitalized psychotic, and asked if they agreed with the diagnosis. Twenty-two did. Twenty-five regarded him as neurotic or character-disordered. Three thought he was mentally healthy. For the balance, the interview was presented in various more innocuous contexts, for example, a job screening. Here, none thought he was psychotic. Thirteen thought he was neurotic or character-disordered. Thirty-seven found him symptom-free.

In a study reported in 1973, David Rosenhan took a more direct approach.[5] He selected eight stable, well-adjusted individuals, all but one in their middle years, all untainted in their histories or lifestyles by any hint of mental illness. They gained entry as patients into twelve different mental hospitals in five states on the East and West coasts by claiming that they had been hearing voices of late, which seemed to say "empty," "hollow," and "thud." The hospitals represented the gamut of types: private, government, and university; well staffed and understaffed; research-oriented and not. In addition to feigning the voices, pseudopatients falsified their names and the five psychologists and physicians in the group falsified their occupations. Otherwise, they behaved in honest and straightforward fashion and, after admittance, maintained that the voices had ceased. The roles they were instructed to play were themselves, as if they had found themselves in the hospital by virtue of some atypical event in their otherwise normal lives and now needed to convince the staff that they were indeed sane. The question Rosenhan asked was: In how many cases would they obtain discharges as such?

The answer was none. All were readily admitted; all but one with diagnoses of paranoid schizophrenia. The minimum period of hospitalization was seven days; the maximum, fifty-two; and the average, nineteen. Each was released with the same diagnosis as upon admission, sometimes with an appendum such as "improved" or "in remission."

Pseudopatients found that virtually every aspect of their behavior could be translated into clinical symptoms. One was approached by a nurse as he paced the corridor – a common response to the tedium of hospital life – who asked him why he was so nervous. Another, waiting with several other patients for the dining room to open, heard a psychiatrist describe them to a group of residents as demonstrating characteristic "oral-acquisitive" tendencies. Three who were taking notes found this entered into their nursing records as signs of obsessiveness or paranoia or the like, though no one had inquired as to the content or purpose of their writing. Reports of clinical interviews were similarly distorted. One pseudopatient had revealed that he had felt closer to his mother than to his father in early childhood but that this was reversed in adolescence; that his wife and he had occasional angry exchanges but that their relationship was generally close and warm and free of friction; and that their children had been rarely spanked. His discharge summary contained the following:

> This white 39 year old male . . . manifests a long history of considerable ambivalence in close relationships, which begins in early childhood. A warm relationship with his mother cools during his adolescence. A distant relationship to his father is described as becoming very intense. Affective stability is absent. His attempts to control emotionality with his wife and children are punctuated by angry outbursts and, in the case of the children, spankings. And while he says that he has several good friends, one senses considerable ambivalence embedded in those relationships, also.

Mental illness is a matter of context: it exists in the eye of the beholder. Once you are believed to be afflicted, there is nothing that you can say or do to establish that you are not, either to a layman or a professional.

It has always been this way. Thomas Szasz uncovered and translated an amusing piece by the early-twentieth-century

Hungarian scholar Frigyes Karinthy.[6] Karinthy immersed himself in books and lectures on psychiatry at the dawn of the modern movement and then prevailed upon a psychiatrist friend to allow him to wander within the local asylum. He describes the moment he decided to "quit mental illness" as when a supposed patient he chatted with, who seemed to him to be a classic paranoid schizophrenic, turned out to be a long-time respected attendant.

Nowadays, attendants wear badges and such errors are rare. But the following is a modern tale, told to me by a student – an original flower-child who still kept his hair long and smiled to strangers – of his visit to a mental hospital to see a friend:

Somehow I got to her room without a visitor's pass, but she wasn't there. Another patient told me she left the hospital, so I started to go, but now the door to the ward was locked. I was standin' there jiggling the handle and a nurse came up to me and asked real sweetly, "Can I help you?" I said, "Yeah, you can open this door," and she said, "Are you a patient?" I couldn't resist. I gave her a big, freak grin and told her "No, I always act this way."

Well, they kept me there for nearly an hour. They wouldn't believe anything I said, and they wouldn't let me go until they checked for a missing patient in every ward of the hospital.

It was incredible. I was in the staff room with a doctor and two nurses. I couldn't sit still, you know, I was nervous and embarrassed. So I fidgeted and kept jumping out of my chair and pacing around, and chewed my thumb like I do when I'm tense. Then, I noticed that they were all looking at me kind of sideways. I thought, "Oh my God, they think I'm acting crazy." So I tried to look real calm and smiled at anyone who looked at me, and they gave me these frozen smiles back – except the doctor, he just stared – and I thought, "This is worse." Then I said, kind of loudly, "Listen, I'm not crazy." They all looked up real quickly. There was a long silence and then the doctor said, really condescending, "No one said that you were. Did they?" The rest of the time I just sat staring at the floor and I *knew* they were convinced, then.

You know, even after they checked me out, I had the feeling they thought I really belonged there. I said to the nurse who opened the door for me, "Well, I'll never go into a mental hospital without a visitor's pass again," and she just raised an eyebrow, like, who did I think I was fooling?

FOUR-FIFTHS OF MIDTOWN MANHATTAN IS MENTALLY ILL

The most revealing testimony to the all-encompassing nature of psychiatric categories came from within the traditional bastions of the field: an epic research published in two volumes in 1962 called, *Mental Health in the Metropolis: The Midtown Manhattan Study*.[7] The main conclusion, from the responses of 1600 residents of the East Side of New York City, was that close to 80 percent suffered symptoms of mental illness; 95 percent among the lower socioeconomic classes. It remains, to this day, one of the most widely cited and acclaimed findings of the mental-health literature. It is analogous to a physician informing a patient that he is dying, and when the patient asks what fatal disease he suffers from, the physician replies, "None in particular; everyone is dying." Of course, to say that someone is dying, in the sense that everyone is, cannot be meaningfully regarded as a medical diagnosis; it is a comment on the human condition. If one were found *not* to be dying, in fact, he might earn the attention of the medical profession. Similarly, to assert that virtually everyone is mentally ill is to say that no one is mentally ill. The one in five who is considered sound may bear watching, however, for how difficult he or she must find this imperfect world.

Despite the data and the critics, including Szasz's prolific, erudite dissents of nearly three decades, the establishment remains unchanged in concept and untarnished in image. Mental illness is consistently ranked by governmental agencies as our most prevalent health problem. Psychiatry maintains it's status as a respected branch of the profession most respected in our society for truth and rigor. In the face of this, can it all be an illusion? How could such an illusion endure? Why would it endure?

It is simpler to repeat conventional wisdom than to try to refute it, and the case must be painstakingly presented. But beforehand, two points should be made clear:

- First, to disavow mental illness is not to deny emotional and behavioral problems. It means, simply that the medical model does not pertain appropriately. Nor does it deny the possibility of remediation. In fact, as we will try to show, the search for valid explanations is in the interests of finding valid modes of helping.

- Second, it is the medical model applied to the diversities of human thought, feeling, and behavior that is taken to task here. Throughout, I refer to it's purveyors, interchangeably, as mental-health professionals or psychiatrists, by which I include anyone who embraces the tenets of the model, in whole or any aspect, whether they are from psychiatry, psychology, nursing, education, or whatever. I have no quarrel with the minority who bear some accoutrements of the model, for example, those who call themselves doctors, but truly disavow the medical approach in their dealings with clientele. Many who *believe* they represent this group, however, may find the need to revise their self-images somewhat as they read through the text.

DOCTORS OF THE MIND:
Metaphysical Abstractions Cannot Become Diseased

THE MEANING OF ILLNESS

Is mental illness really illness? That is, is it a conceptually valid subcategory of illness proper?

An unambiguous definition of illness is not easy to come by. Dictionaries tend to define it in the negative; for example, "the absence of health," or "an unsound condition of the body." The former begs the question entirely, since health is generally defined as the absence of illness; the latter fails to exclude such states as fatigue, dissipation, or insobriety. I heard Szasz give the following definition: "Illness is something a person can have and his corpse can have it also." [1] He went on to say that the only diseases corpses cannot have are those that aren't really diseases: schizophrenia, homosexuality, phobias, and so on. Szasz's statement was succinct and to the point, but insubstantial for the present purposes.

Physicians whom I've asked have given unqualified approval to the following definition: "An illness is an abnormality of some bodily part or process, associated with functional impairment." Both components—abnormality and impairment—are necessary to the definition. A person may be abnormally tall or short or have an abnormally high or low sperm count or metabolic rate without being functionally impaired and, thereby, ill. By the same token, arteries harden naturally during the life span, joints increase in inflammatory potential, visual acuity decreases, but we do not

9

regard these impairments as illnesses unless they deviate from some norm for the person's age group.

Given that bodies are basically the same – they work in the same ways, respond in the same manner to the same internal and external events – categories of illness are, with remote exceptions, universal. An ulcer is an ulcer, in a man or a woman, in Newfoundland or New Guinea, in the sixteenth century or the twentieth. It can be diagnosed and treated without regard to race, creed, education, socioeconomic class, values, moral convictions, or the like. It is this objectivity and universality that separates medicine from metaphysics, that invests it with its status as science. Though individual physicians may and do disagree about specific cases or conditions, they are able to specify the bases of their disagreements and establish empirical means to resolve their questions.

IS MY SEX DRIVE TOO HIGH?

Mental illness implies abnormality as well; in fact, it is often used synonymously with "abnormal behavior" and "abnormal psychology." It is mainly on this basis that the term is invoked as a category of illness. But when we compare the concept of abnormality as it is used in mental and somatic medicine, we are struck by a gross, irredeemable difference. Designations of "abnormal" in regard to somatic ills represent deviations from known parameters for optimal function. The physician bases his diagnoses on whether such variables as cell count, blood pressure, and body temperature, fall within certain sets of absolute values. Such values do not exist for mental or emotional or behavioral variables. We cannot say, for example, how much intelligence, or aggression, or conformity, or sexuality represent optimal amounts. The questions themselves seem foolish for the reason that, whereas bodily processes are notably homogeneous, the hallmark of personality and behavioral variables is their diversity. The standard we might establish for aggression for middle-class Americans will certainly not pertain to Zulu tribesmen. The values we assign for solitude and introversion may apply to monks or to salesmen but certainly not to both.

Abnormality in the definition of mental illness refers not to comparisons with established standards, but to comparisons of an individual with other individuals. Inasmuch as norms for behavior differ markedly among cultures and subcultures, the comparison group is necessarily the small segment of society with which the person is identified, although often, I have found, it is the small segment of society with which the diagnostician is identified. For example, a lady described to me her total inability to convince a psychiatrist who had come from an overtly male-dominant culture that her conflict with her husband about her decision to resume her career was the cause and not the symptom of her depression. A rock-ribbed, conservative, rural-Midwestern psychiatrist of my acquaintance, who came to a large, Eastern city, was shocked at the widespread "sociopathy" of welfare cheats. He found it difficult to assimilate the fact that among the metropolitan poor, this bordered on the norm. Needless to say, in medicine proper, where abnormality is absolute, the cultural background and social attitudes of the physician are of no consequence.

The public, even the most enlightened sector, seems oblivious to this critical distinction. Mental-health professionals are routinely asked questions such as: "Is my child *too* shy?"; "Is my sex drive *too* high or low?"; "Am I *too* sensitive?", as if the good doctors had tables to refer to, similar to blood pressure or cell count. Of course, the public remains oblivious because mental-health professionals answer them as if they had such tables. Psychiatry and psychology comport themselves as if their clinical categories were derived from identifiable abnormalities within the nervous system. The field is rife with pseudo-organic jargon; for example, *minimal brain dysfunction, hyperkinesis, senile dementia, neurasthenia, hypomania, involutional melancholia,* all calculated to convey the impression of measurable neurological entities.

More than one million children in North America are diagnosed "hyperkinetic" or some equivalent [2] and are treated with powerful drugs on a sustained basis simply because they have been deemed *too* active. Too active for what? And for whom? The confinement of an urban classroom? The restrictive routines of apartment dwellers? There are no organic correlates for hyperkinesis, despite the connotation of the label. Nor is there, nor could we conceive, a universal behavioral standard for children's activity levels.

Similarly, an estimated five and one-half million persons in the United States are considered to be afflicted with "mental retardation," which has been ranked fourth in prevalence among all diseases.[3] For the overwhelming majority of these cases, the "border-line" and "mild" categories that the "cultural-familial" type comprises, the diagnosis is based primarily or solely on some test of Intelligence Quotient (IQ). IQ is a standardized score, which means, in essence, that the raw score is converted to a percentile, and the conversion tables are periodically revised, based on the performances of current samples, so that the proportion of the population in each score category remains constant. There will always be the same proportion of geniuses, the same proportion of normals, the same proportion of retardates. No conceivable research or therapy program can reduce the prevalence of this "disease" in its major form. It can only be attenuated in the manner it was created, by statisticians.

DISEASES OF THE BRAIN VS. DISEASES OF THE MIND

To be sure, there are conditions based on specifiable organic abnormalities that impair the structure and function of the brain and that may directly affect mental capacities and behavior. Included are disorders such as Down's syndrome and phenylketonuria, which account for the approximate five percent of retardates in the "severe" and "profound" categories; brain infections such as cerebral syphilis and epidemic encephalitis; brain tumors; head injuries that result in lacerations, contusions, or hemorrhaging of the brain; cerebral arteriosclerosis; and certain toxic and metabolic disturbances.

The paradox is that all such conditions are in the domains of medical specialities other than psychiatry: neurology for the most part, though childhood illnesses are generally the province of pediatricians, and metabolic disturbances are dealt with by internists. Most of these diseases are listed in the nomenclature of the American Psychiatric Association under the classification "Organic Brain Syndromes" and one will occasionally find cases in psychiatric wards receiving custodial care, but the skills and responsibilities for diagnoses and treatments reside elsewhere.

There are, however, other conditions listed in the psychiatric nomenclature as Organic Brain Syndromes that belong exclusively to psychiatry and that illuminate the peculiar selectivity of this profession. These are "make-believe" organic diseases. *Senile dementia*, the disease of growing old, is one. Organic in name only, the diagnosis is not based on neurological tests of any kind, and post-mortem studies have failed to find any correlation with brain damage.[4] *Postpartum psychosis* is another that casts as an organic affliction any extreme expression of the conflict and anxiety that some women feel initially toward motherhood. Finally, there are a number of psychiatric patients who bear the label Organic Brain Syndrome, "unspecified" or "undifferentiated," which means that they seem to behave in some respects like people with organic disorders, but their neurological examinations have revealed no such condition. Consider the status of a medical science in which the physician's initial diagnosis is sustained, regardless of the results of laboratory tests, simply because there is no other label to apply.

Though psychiatrists labor to have us believe otherwise, so-called diseases of the mind and diseases of the brain are very distinct entities, and the discrepancies exist by their own design. Psychiatry has forsaken the brain in favor of the mind, but "brain" refers to an organ of the body and "mind" to a metaphysical abstraction invoked to enable contemplation and discourse on the myriad diversity of human thoughts, feelings, and actions. Organs of the body can become diseased; metaphysical abstractions cannot. A person may say of another, "He has a sick mind," to imply that the other thinks or acts in ways that are outside of the ken of comprehension of the observer or are unacceptable by his own social or moral standards, but he is aware that he speaks in metaphor and not medicine. Psychiatrists and psychologists do not use the term "sick mind"; they speak instead of "mental illness," but they are perfect synonyms.

MENTAL HEALTH ACCORDING
TO THE MIDDLE CLASS

Still to be considered is the second requirement for the definition of illness. Abnormality, per se, is not a sufficient condition for illness in regard to somatic variables and it is apparent that this holds as true for mental or emotional or behavioral traits. Inasmuch as variations in these traits do not customarily foretell physical impairment, the question remains as to what criteria shall serve to separate those abnormalities that qualify as mental illness and those that do not. How will we define the state of behavioral impairment?

To describe the state of impairment, we must first be able to describe the state of nonimpairment, a task that requires a clear idea of the function or purpose of whatever is in question. For bodily organs and systems, these are generally apparent: the function of the lungs is to take in oxygen; of the eyes to see. But what is the purpose of thought, or emotions, or behavior? What are correct attitudes, proper feelings, right ways to live? There are, of course, as many answers as there are divergent personal and social value systems, and there are, always have been, and, it is to be hoped, always will be many divergent personal and social value systems. So-called universal definitions of mental health are, ultimately, reflections of these.

For example, the most widely repeated viewpoint, by psychologist Joseph Shoben, maintains that the five "universal" qualities of mental health are: self-control, personal responsibility, social responsibility, democratic social consciousness, and ideals.[5] Of course, these also represent the embodiment of middle-class, academic values, and thus cast, as the epitome of mental health, psychiatrists, psychologists, and other bright, successful, conventional types espousing liberal ideals. All who depart from the mode are suspect: hedonists, adventurers, free spirits, rebels, any who flout traditional lifestyles and morality. However, *these* are usually our romantic heros and heroines, not self-controlled, responsible achievers, a paradox that probably reflects ambivalences within middle-class society about its' own conventions.

Included, as well, in the unhealthy category are the masses: the "also-rans" in the Great Western Competition for status and resources. What expressions of social responsibility and democratic social consciousness shall be expected of someone whose energies are consumed eking out the bare means to exist? These are the folks to whom such platitudes are directed. Democratic social consciousness for this group means, in fact, extracting a larger share of the pie from their more favored brethren – including those who invent class-conscious definitions of mental health for their ample livelihoods – and it is certainly to be expected that they may lose their ideals and, occassionally, their self-control in the frustration of the attempt.

Such definitions help clarify the process by which the Midtown Study found symptoms of mental illness in 95 percent of a lower socioeconomic sample.

Some views are even more blatantly value-laden than these. Coleman's abnormal-psychology text, probably the most widely used throughout its five editions, defines healthy behavior as behavior that "fosters the well-being of the individual and ultimately the group." As illustrations of unhealthy behavior we find: ". . . prejudice and discrimination against persons because of race or sex, wasteful use of our natural resources, pollution of our air and water, irrational violence and political corruption."[6]

Of course, different social and political systems will have different definitions of mental health, which was aptly demonstrated in the much-publicized, passionate controversy of the mid-1970s between Western and Soviet psychiatrists. Perhaps blissfully unmindful of the sociopolitical nature of their own concepts, Western psychiatrists were shocked by the discovery that their Soviet counterparts were routinely diagnosing mental illness on the basis of such acts as resigning from the Communist party on religious grounds or reading anti-Marxist poetry to friends,[8] and brought a motion before the World Psychiatric Association in 1977 to censure such practices as abuses of psychiatry. By the same token, the Soviets' responses of puzzled innocence were probably just as naive and sincere. The confusion of the profession-at-large to this revelation of its own folly was reflected in the vote on the censure motion, which passed by the barest margin of 90 to 88.

Mental illness is not illness, in any but a purely figurative sense. It is a metaphor, with no more meaning, medically, than "illness of the soul" or "economic ills" or "ill tempered." But we are not generally misled by metaphor. No one would think of calling the fire department to deal with a burning issue, or the police to a stock market crash. Why do we seek physicians to cure sick minds? For the answer we must explore the ideological nature and purpose of the mental-illness metaphor.

PSYCHOFASCISM:
Politics of the
Mental-Health Movement

SEMINAR IN A MADHOUSE

At one point in my research, I gained access to several mental hospitals and wards in order to simply wander about, like Karinthy, talking to patients. I found that they usually welcomed me as a potential relief from the tedium of the day, and I had little problem gathering groups together for spontaneous discussions. My questions were: How did you get into the hospital? What has happened to you here? How do you feel about it? The following is from my transcription of one of these seminars in 1978, in a large state institution where most patients were involuntary.

Frank: [He is about 45, wears a wrinkled pinstriped suit, speaks with no attempt to conceal his anger.] I was picked up at the goddamned railroad station. Just got into town from up north . . . picked me up and brought me here.

Dr. S: What were you doing? Who picked you up?

Frank: I wasn't doin' nothin'. Fuckin' cops picked me up. I was goin' up to people and talkin' to 'em . . . tryin' to find out where I could stay cheap . . . get a job . . . you know? Didn't know anyone here. I was tryin' to make some contacts. Fuckin' cops ask me where I live . . . what I was doin' here . . . smelled

my breath. I had two beers in the station. I got
mad . . . told them I didn't commit no crime. So
they say I'm being a public nuisance and take me
in. Spent the night in the fuckin' jail. Next day they
bring me here. Been here for a goddamned month
and a half.

Dr. S: Have you seen a doctor?

Frank: Yeah. Fuckin' doctor sent for me after three
days . . . for about ten goddamned minutes. Never
saw him again.

Dr. S: What did he ask you?

Frank: What month it was. What day it was. Count back-
wards from 100. Why I didn't have a job. How
much I drank. So I lost my temper, you know. Told
him he's got to let me out . . . I'm not crazy. So he
says we'll find out . . . that I'm gonna stay thirty
days at least and I better cool down and behave.
Never saw him again.

Dr. S: Have you seen anyone else?

Frank: Yeah. Everyday some doctor comes around here.
Walks around. Sometimes the same one, some-
times different. I always ask them . . . when the
hell am I gonna get out o' here? They tell me . . .
when we decide . . . when you're ready. Sometimes
they don't even answer me. Just walk away.

Tom: [He is in his early twenties, long hair, wears a
T-shirt and faded jeans; trim and muscular.] Let
me ask you somethin', man. Like I'm in here for
drugs . . . right? So all they do is give me drugs.
How's that supposed to help me?

Dr. S: How did you get in here?

Tom: I was partyin' . . . doin' acid. I guess I had a bad
trip . . . started screamin' or somethin'. They said I
wasn't makin' sense, but I don't remember much.
Anyway, this dumb shit girlfriend of mine gets

scared. Takes me to a hospital. They put me to sleep with somethin' and next morning I'm O.K. I tell them I wanna go home. I tell them I'm goin' off the stuff. I wasn't kidding, man. I ain't goin' near it again. They tell me I gotta come here for a while. It's been three fuckin' weeks. All they do is keep me stoned. Like, is that gonna help me?

Dr. S: Does a doctor see you?

Tom: Just the ones who come around. Like they ask me how I feel and write something down. I heard they get $20 for each of us each time they come around here. Is that so? I figure they make $400 for just walkin' around for an hour.

Dr. S: I don't know what they make, but it could be something like that.

Howard: [He is standing in the rear of the group.] Do you think we're crazy?

Dr. S: No I don't.

Howard: Then why are we here?

Dr. S: [after a pause] I don't have a simple answer to that. These two just seemed to be in the wrong place at the wrong time. How did you get here?

Howard: [He pulls a chair close to me; talks in low tones. He is about 30, neatly dressed, intense, and articulate.] Do you know any of the doctors at the Community Hospital? [I gesture that I don't.] Well, I was head storekeeper there for five years. That's a very responsible job. I mean it doesn't require much education, but there's a lot you have to know and you can't make mistakes and I did very well. But I'd get depressed every once in a while. Especially about my job. I thought I could do better. I took some night courses at the college and I did O.K., but I couldn't really get into anything. Do you know what I mean? [I nod.] So I went to a psychiatrist and he put me on lithium carbonate and that made me feel better for awhile, but then I became more depressed. I think it was the drug. I didn't want to leave the house, even to go to work. So my mother insisted I go back to the psychiatrist and he suggested that I go into the N.P. [neuropsychiatric] ward. He said they'd only keep me a few days. Well, I did. And I flipped out there. . . .

Dr. S: What do you mean, you flipped out? What did you do?

Howard: Oh, I kicked a door . . . shouted at a nurse a couple of times, that's all. I'm not violent. I guess I felt I could express my feelings there.

Dr. S: What happened then?

Howard: They transferred me here and I've been here for over three months. I can't get out unless my mother says she wants me back, and she thinks I'm really sick. She says the psychiatrist . . . the one I went to . . . told her that if they're keeping me here they've got good reason.

Dr. S: Are you getting any medical attention?

Howard: Pills every day. I think they're phenothiazines, but no one will tell me. I don't want to take them. I don't like what they do to me and I know about the side effects. I refused to take them once and the nurse said that if I didn't, they'd give it to me by injection.

Dr. S: Did you see a doctor?

Howard: The psychiatrist who does rounds most of the time, Dr. _____, he saw me in his office twice. He said I wasn't a depressive; I was a schizophrenic. He said that I probably was since birth . . . that it was a genetic disease . . . and that when I left the hospital I'd have to continue taking drugs to control it all of my life . . . like a diabetic. Do you believe that? I don't believe that.

Dr. S:	What do you believe is your problem?
Howard:	I've just got to straighten my life out. Find some direction . . . get out of my mother's house. But I don't know how I'm going to do that if I can't get out of here. This place is making me crazy.
Dr. S:	You came into the hospital voluntarily. Why don't you just leave? [I suspect the answer.]
Howard:	[excited] I tried that. Told them I was going. The head nurse said that if I tried to leave they would change my status to involuntary and then it would be even harder to get discharged. Then I asked the doctor and he said yes, they will. Can you imagine that?
Dr. S:	Yes, I'm afraid I can. I hope that you can convince your mother to ask for your release.
Howard:	If I do . . . when I get out of here, I'll never go near a psychiatrist again. I don't care how depressed I get.
Frank:	[smirking] Why don't you talk to Jeff over there. He's got a good story. [He points to a man in his twenties standing outside of the group, who had been listening without expression but watching me intently. He wears an Indian madras shirt and jeans, hair to his shoulders, and a full, neatly trimmed beard.]
Dr. S:	Do you want to tell me your story?
Jeff:	[His eyes shine more brightly than any of the rest and he speaks slowly. I suspect he's on maximum dosage.] Are you a psychologist? [I nod.] Do you believe in astral projection? [There are smiles from some of the other patients.]
Dr. S:	Well, I haven't thought much about it. I know some people who do.
Jeff:	[He seems satisfied with this and moves closer.] I projected myself into a space/time warp, once. . . .

	Do you know what that is? [I nod.] And I lived a future life, I was a psychologist.
Dr. S:	That sounds interesting. What do psychologists do in the future?
Jeff:	[more animated now] Well, drugs are out. So is psychoanalysis. All the Freud stuff. Everything is done by changing brain waves with laser beams. However you want to change a person, there's a way to change his brain waves to do it.
Dr. S:	How did you get into this hospital?
Jeff:	My wife . . . I'm married, but we fight all of the time. We're not spiritually compatible. It's just a physical relationship. Are you married? [I nod.] Are you spiritually compatible with your wife?
Dr. S:	I think so, but I'd like to know how you got here.
Jeff:	I left her after a fight. She called the police and told them I was crazy and I threatened to come back and kill her. It was bullshit. I never hurt a living thing. I may have stepped on an insect without knowing it but if I see an insect, I'll walk around it. They have spiritual lives too, you know.
Dr. S:	Did the police find you and pick you up?
Jeff:	Yeah. They took me to the general hospital . . . to the emergency room. I waited there with a policeman guarding me for two hours. He even stayed with me in the doctor's office. I don't know if the doctor was a psychiatrist or a psychologist. I asked him, but he wouldn't tell me.
Dr. S:	What did the doctor talk to you about?
Jeff:	He asked me if I threatened my wife. I told him, no way . . . that *she* was really crazy. She is. She's paranoid.
Dr. S:	Anything else?

Jeff:	Yeah. He asked me if it was true that I thought I lived in the future, and that I saw spirits. I guess he got all that from my wife.
Dr. S:	And you told him you did?
Jeff:	Yeah. [frowns] I probably never should've done that.
Dr. S:	How long have you been here?
Jeff:	Five and a half months.
Dr. S:	Do you still tell doctors about astral projection and spirits?
Jeff:	They don't ask me anymore.

THE SHADOW STATE

In the eyes of psychiatry, these are four sufferers of psychosis, all certifiable by reasons of their mental illnesses and their consequent potential dangerousness to themselves or others. In actuality, we have a vagabond, a hippie, a mama's boy, and a streetcorner metaphysician. All are sufferers indeed, but of the covert, omnipresent fascism within our society that masquerades as the mental-health movement. An ideology that mainly serves the socially and economically more powerful at the expense of the less, it is used routinely by husbands against wives, occasionally by wives against husbands, by both parents against young children and grown children against aged parents, by arbiters of social custom against transgressors, and by civil authorities at every level as an expedient, extralegal device for social control. It is a shadow state, offering all of the convenience of totalitarianism while maintaining the illusion of political democracy. It is so pervasive that, at last count, twice as many Americans were incarcerated by its jurisdiction than by the legal system proper.[1]

In authoritarian settings, where the arbitrary exercise of power is unencumbered by democratic considerations and where social custom is overtly mandated and enforced, psychiatry has very little role. The Shanghai Mental Hospital with one hundred beds serves a population of more than ten million people and its medical director has declared that "in the People's Republic, mental illness is simply not a problem." [2] Similarly, as archives discovered by Szasz have revealed,[3] in the mid-nineteenth century, the proportion of blacks to whites institutionalized for insanity was low in slave states and high in free states.

Somewhere in our consciousness we must, at least, strongly suspect all of this, for the true nature of the system surfaces often enough. The New York *Times* report of the transcripts of David Frost's interviews with Richard Nixon in 1977 [4] contained statements by the former president that strongly implied that Martha Mitchell, a vociferous critic of Nixon's administration with access to incriminating information, was detained in a mental institution to silence her during the 1968 presidential campaign. Attorney Bruce Ennis's *Prisoners of Psychiatry*, which has gone through several printings, describes dozens of less infamous cases equally blatant in their abuses.[5] So, too, quite frequently, do the daily newspapers. The following four cases are summarized from a newspaper's recent investigative report: [6]

- A young wife was escorted by her husband to the emergency room of a general hospital for an intense headache following a heated domestic quarrel. The husband told the physician that his wife had a tendency to become hysterical, whereupon she was placed in the psychiatric ward and there remained, under duress, for six weeks.
- A father threatened two men, who were reputed to be leaders of a prostitution and drug ring, with a weapon when he discovered his runaway, minor daughter was in their company. Upon his arrest, he expressed to the police his intention to complain formally about their lack of effort to find his daughter. A psychiatrist who interviewed him reported that he suffered "paranoia and delusions," which referred, respectively, to his attitude toward the police and his belief (notwithstanding the fact that it was accurate) that his daughter was among pimps and pushers. He was remanded to a mental institution for five and one-half months prior to his trial.
- A twenty-nine-year-old teacher who often chagrinned his parents by his counterculture ways, embarked to live in a tent, in the woods, for a summer by himself. At the request of a psychiatrist solicited by his parents, he was taken from his tent to a mental hospital and confined for thirty days.
- A middle-aged man became upset at his wife's psychiatrist and wrote

her a letter in which he used the unfortunate phrase, "there might be a bit of buckshot flying around Mission [the name of their town]." The day the letter arrived he was taken by police to a mental institution, not to emerge for five months.

If these cases were unusual enough to earn media attention, it was only because the victims were of higher than typical socio-economic status and had the external resources to facilitate their escapes.

But where were the voices of outraged protest at these publicly exposed miscarriages of civil rights and medical ethics? Are we so oblivious to gross violations of humanity and justice within our midst? Not ordinarily, but we are, most of us, part of the plot. Psychiatry provides the ideology and performs as gatekeeper, for high compensation in status and stipend, but it is the mainstream of society that is served by the system. The service is provided in two related, but distinctive, ways:

- First, it permits the rapid isolation, control, and punishment of anyone who violates local tradition or order, in any manner, in the public or private domain; people, as in the examples above, who disrupt the harmony of their households, reject the lifestyles of their families and communities, come into conflict, justifiably or not, with police or other civil authorities, or, horror of horrors, directly offend the psychiatric demagogues themselves.
- Second, it provides the justification and means for the covert propagation of certain specific societal aims and standards. To appreciate in full this second function, we must return to a prior question: What criteria serve to separate those traits or behaviors for which abnormality represents illness rather than inter-individual differences? We have witnessed the failure to pose an objective, universal standard. Now, let us see what happens in actual practice.

WILLFUL CHILDREN, SLOW LEARNERS, AND OLD PEOPLE

Consider the disorder of *hyperkinesis*, or *hyperactivity* as it is often called. The diagnosis generally begins with the complaint of the classroom teacher about a child, usually male, who cannot (or *will* not, which is more to the point) "sit still" or "be silent" or "do what he is supposed to do." No one who has attended a traditional elementary school will fail to recognize the affliction, perhaps in themselves, but if not in themselves, certainly with empathy. For it is not that the rest of us were having a joyful and fulfilling experience; indeed, it required a good deal of restraint to keep our bodies and minds precisely where the curriculum demanded they be kept for hours on end.

Before the emergence of hyperkinesis, "willful" was the term for those who could not or would not, or "high energy," depending on one's benevolence toward children. In my generation, they were appointed monitors of all sorts and were kept hustling to the roof to clean blackboard erasers or to other rooms to deliver messages, or they were broken to the rules by whatever intimidation was necessary, or they were simply tolerated. Then how did it suddenly become illness, for the category came into wide use just a dozen or so years ago? There were no discoveries of pathological biological states associated with unusual energy or willfulness. Perhaps it had more to do with the introduction of automatic eraser cleaners and electronic communication systems.

Journalists Peter Schrag and Diane Divocky [7] have traced the origin of the movement to the pharmaceutical industry, which discovered an expedient and highly profitable means to restrain children who do not conform well to confinement and discipline. But the means are harsh indeed. The modal treatment for hyperkinesis is prolonged administration of an amphetamine-type drug called Ritalin ®. This does render children more manageable and probably increases their attentional capacities for routine tasks, much as any variety of "speed" does for college students, who sometimes use it to cram for exams, or housewives, some of whom use it to get through long days of tedious routines. Aside from the moral issue of drug programs for children who are not ill, the constant intake of Ritalin causes a multitude of adverse, extraneous, short-term effects, and it's long-term side effects have not yet been ascertained. [8]

The drug companies, however, could not have done it alone. The hyperkinesis-Ritalin movement was probably an insidious reaction to the revolution of the 1960s within our universities and elsewhere, tumultuous confrontations between generations across barriers of armed police and National Guardsmen. Possibly the temper of conservative, adult society became receptive to the advent of ultraeffective controls for the nonconforming, very young: a cunning, sweeping deterrent to the development of radical leaders of the next generation, without cost to democratic ideals or personal conscience.

Is there a real phenomenon of hyperkinesis? Submerged among the hundreds of thousands whose illness is merely that their behaviors disrupt the schedules of their relatively *hypo*active adult authorities, are there children who live in near constant states of diffuse, agitated motion, irrespective of circumstance — states that the professionals would have us believe are prototypical of the condition?

Descriptions of the disorder have existed for more than 100 years, suggesting that there is some validity to the category. Whenever I have counselled parents or other concerned adults about a child who has been given the label and the drug, I ask whether the hyperactivity is "situational": is the child distressed or disruptive all of the time, or only at school or when he is coerced to do something he doesn't want to do? Are there activities, such as sports or hobbies or TV, that he can partake in for prolonged periods without problems? One time, in the dozens of times I've asked these questions, I received a reply suggesting generalized agitation. Among the thirty or so children that I observed directly who bore the label, I found one who might have qualified. I queried several professionals with sentiments similar to my own, who work exclusively with children, and they concurred that one or two of every hundred diagnosed cases probably refer to actual hyperkinesis.

In regard to these rare, real cases, one pediatrician maintains that those he has seen have shown, with careful examination, some underlying medical cause; for example, reduced oxygenation due to a heart defect in one case, an abnormal glucose level associated with prediabetes in another.[9] Thus the mental-illness ideology may have two sets of victims in this instance: the offenders to adult controls and discipline who are the actual targets, and some truly ill children who are, inadvertently, never properly diagnosed.

We see a very similar application of the ideology in the diagnoses of borderline and mild mental retardation, which compose the vast class of so-called mental defectives often referred to as "cultural-familial" types. Again the process almost invariably begins in the schools. The diagnosis is based always on an IQ score, often supplemented by teachers' reports of less than optimal classroom performance. The fact that these criteria are related is to be expected. IQ tests are designed to measure specific abilities that foretell academic success, and only this circumscribed aspect of the global qualities commonly defined as "intelligence." There are issues about the validity of the test for even this limited purpose, but, this aside, the question for our present argument is why this particular individual difference has come to be regarded as a disease. Why not focus on musical or athletic abilities? The answer is that the labelling of below-average students as diseased or medically defective provides both the means and the justification to isolate them in special classrooms or schools. We thereby assure that they will not impede the scheduled progress of the mainstream through the public-education curriculum, and we spare the system the burden and expense of expanding the concept of education to one of serving the diversity of needs and talents and dispositions of all children. David Saunders and I discovered that institutionalization rates for retardates across geographical areas varied markedly in inverse proportion to the per capita funds available for public education,[10] and studies of institutionalized, cultural-familial retardates by Dorothea and Benjamin Braginsky revealed that, in terms of a more holistic definition of intelligence than IQ score or classroom grades, these children equal and, in some ways, surpass their "mentally healthy" counterparts.[11] The fact that the great majority of such children come from the politically less-influential, lower socioeconomic classes allows the practice to persist unchallenged.

As the mental-retardation metaphor enables us to isolate problem children, the concept of *senile dementia* accomplishes the same function in regard to problem elders. Ontogeny, the life cycle of an individual, is a chronology of mental and behavioral progressions that, for those who are fortunate enough to attend all, can be delineated into four epochs: infancy, childhood, adulthood, and old age. Similar to most dimensions of human development and behavior (simple reflexes may be the exceptions) inter-individual variations are the hallmark, both in terms of the timing and of the extent of these progressions. To create a disease of such variations for any one epoch has as much rationale as for any other epoch. To regard as ill those who live long enough to show changes associated with old age or those for whom this progression is more rapid or extensive is as meaningful, medically, as applying the label to an unusually mature child.[12] But as part of psychofascism, it makes much sense, for it enables the expeditious dispensation of another segment of surplus population. Virtually all of the hundreds of thousands of elderly people confined to mental hospitals with senile dementia are there involuntarily. Many are committed by the actions of family: some well-intentioned, seeking proper care and treatment, though, of course, there is no treatment for aging minds, nor care, beyond compassion and tolerance. Some families are less well-intentioned, for it is far easier on the conscience to institutionalize someone because he is ill than because he is burdensome; and some are blatantly ill-intentioned, taking advantage of a convenient route to premorbid inheritance. Others become labelled and committed simply because they are a nuisance to their neighbors or because they are without resources for self-care. A humanistic society may wish to make provisions for its destitute aged, just as it provides for destitute children, but the imposition of psychiatry in the process is as superfluous in the former instance as in the latter, and is generally injurious to the subject for whom a total institution is usually an unnecessary and nonoptimal resolution.

A MEDICAL-SCIENTIFIC VICE SQUAD

Sex. No other topic earns nearly as much attention by mental-health professionals and no other profession has nearly as much to say about it. Though this is commonly attributed to the Freudian tradition, Freud, in fact, was concerned with untoward effects of repressive sexual attitudes, while psychiatrists and psychologists today are the watchdogs of conventional morality: A medical-scientific vice squad. They conjure symptoms or diseases for virtually every aspect of human sexuality that does not conform to traditional standards.

Let a woman reveal sexual missteps, past or present, in a clinical interview, and it will come to occupy a prominent place in her diagnosis. I have asked scores of young women about their psychiatric histories, and the most commonly-occurring event that led to their initial encounter with the mental health establishment was parental objection to adolescent sexual proclivities. Oddly enough, from a medical, but not an ideological standpoint, I have never encountered a male who had been referred for psychiatric assessment because of higher-than-average sexual activity. The psychiatric nosology, which defines *nymphomania* as "pathologically excessive sexual desire in a female," does not even have a counterpart term for the male.

As further illustration, consider *hysterical personality disorder*, defined as, "emotional instability, overreaction, self-dramatization, egocentricity, and dependence on others." Until a few decades ago, that description was formally regarded as exclusively female and, in practice, this has hardly changed. Thus we find, in a popular, contemporary text: "The classic example of this personality disorder is the hysterical female who apparently lacks awareness of her effect on others and is usually seductive towards males, including the therapist. The sensuous voice and suggestive manner of dress often belie the frigidity and shallowness of her personal relationships, and although much is promised, little is given." As if it is not yet evident whose "emotional instability, overreaction, and egocentricity" is at stake, the paragraph concludes, ". . . therapists for this disorder often maintain that a 'good screw' will suffice." [13]

The pervasiveness of psychiatric judgments by sex-role stereotypes was neatly demonstrated by Inge Broverman and her colleagues in a study reported in 1970. Seventy-nine psychiatric practitioners (46 men and 33 women) were divided into three groups. All used identical rating scales but the instructions varied. Each group was assigned to characterize one of the following: Either "a mature, healthy, socially competent adult male," "female," or "person." Profiles of the healthy male were largely similar to those of the healthy person, but the mentally sound female was seen as, "more submissive, less independent, more easily excitable in minor crises, having their feelings more easily hurt, more conceited about their appearance, less objective and disliking math and science." Interestingly, these differences were similar for male and female clinicians.[14]

When there are considerations beyond the perpetuation of sex-role typing, however, the focus can turn on the male. Whether it is by inherent biological differences, or by their historically greater latitude for expression, the male of the species seems to show more of the odd turns and quirks and exotic variations that humankind's vast potential for sexual experience comprises: *deviations* in the clinical term. But which of these deviations turn up in the diagnostic manuals, and which do not?

Consider *pedophilia*, a typically male phenomenon. There is no basis in medical science to regard as a clinical entity those whose sexual preferences range to the young as opposed to the old, or to focus on variations in age preference rather than any other type of preference – physiognomy of partner, or foreplay ritual, for example. One could list deviations from common practice for virtually any aspect of sexuality and, in the process, encounter a variety that most people would find unfathomable and/or repugnant. Why don't these find their way into the psychiatric lexicon, as well? The adult who is attracted to the very young is distinct because he is potentially dangerous. Similarly, there is no reason to separate, medically, men who surreptitiously observe females undressing from their numerous brethren who enjoy undressing rituals by their partners or in strip shows, except that the so-called "sufferer" of *voyeurism* is a public nuisance. Nor is the male afflicted with *exhibitionism* distinguishable on medical grounds from the female who dresses to expose as much breast and buttock as the law will allow, though he is by societal standards that govern the expression of such inclinations.

But there are criminal laws governing such matters. Why have "psychiatric law"? It is because psychiatric law has the capability of being far more punitive to the transgressor and protective of society than reasonable application of common law would allow. Could we obtain indefinite sentences, which are often life sentences, for exhibitionists or voyeurs or even child molesters? The offender who is tried by mental-health professionals rather than a judge or jury is subject to this fate. (The processes will be described in Chapter 9.) The ideology is ideally suited to a society which is torn between a penchant for equitable justice and a profound distaste for sexual misfits.

We could continue the questions. Why do we have as a major category of mental illness affinity for or dependence on alcohol, and not on nicotine or sugar? (Now that smoking has fallen into social disfavor, however, it is included in the revised Diagnostic and Statistical Manual of the American Psychiatric Association.) Why do we label as personality disordered the so-called compulsive gambler and not the compulsive mountain climber, and why is the label not applied to the inveterate stock-market or real-estate speculator? The habitual imbiber (and now, smoker) is distinctive because he is a potential nuisance or danger. The race-track buff does not engage in the modes of financial risk-taking sanctioned by the prevailing class. Inexorably, the distinctions are explicable only in terms of social control, never in terms of medical science.

Thus, both facets of psychofascism are encompassed in our classifications of mental illness. There are categories defining specific populations who obstruct some social goal or violate some norm: drinkers, voyeurs, sexually intimidating women, children who do not keep the pace or discipline of the classroom. And there are categories sufficiently vague and flexible like *schizophrenia* or *personality disorder*, to deal with anyone else.

FROM DEMONS TO VIRUSES:
Two Interpretations of the
Conceptual Transition from
Witchcraft to Mental Illness

WITCH AS MISDIAGNOSED MENTAL PATIENT

The origins of contemporary psychiatry reside in the 500-year era of witchcraft. This is not a slur. Noone questions the fact of the succession; it is stated, proudly, in every psychiatric and psychology textbook. There are, however, two interpretations of the nature of the transition. The official history of the field maintains that it was based on enlightenment. The modern mental-health movement originated with the revelation that the victims of the inquisitions were not possessed by demons, but by mental illness. Szasz[1] has a different theory.

First, he points out some incongruities of the traditional view with the facts of the inquisitions. The assumption that witches were misdiagnosed mental cases ignores the theological and political nature of the movement, the calculated program of intimidation by which the church maintained its powers in the affairs of state and assured adherence by the masses to its spiritual and social proscriptions. Its victims were, mainly, Catholics in Protestant lands, Protestants in Catholic lands, atheists, heretics, and Jews in any land, and an abundance of women who were allegedly or found to be in violation of the patriarchal moral codes of the times (which included proscriptions of the practices of midwifery, astrology, herb medicine, and such, in addition to the more mundane transgressions). Mental illness, then, would have had to have been a highly sociopolitically-selective affliction.

It is truly remarkable how oblivious contemporary scholars can be to the illogic revealed by Szasz. For example, one modern text quotes the *Malleus Maleficarum*, the authoritative source throughout most of Europe for the detection and remediation of witchcraft, as follows: "All witchcraft comes from carnal lust, which is in women insatiable," and, ". . . three general vices appear to have special dominion over wicked women, namely, infidelity, ambition, and lust. Therefore they are more than others inclined toward witchcraft. . . ." The authors proceed to describe the recommendation of the *Malleus*, that: ". . . the witch be stripped, with her pubic hair shaved, before presentation to the judges, so that demons could not have a place to hide. . . ."[2]

But in the same section of the text, the victims of the *Malleus* are referred to as, "*psychotic* women, who openly expressed erotic fantasies and who blasphemed against the Church" (italics mine).

Szasz argues, further, that although the poor creatures found shackled in dungeons at the close of the inquisitions showed confusion, despair, and a host of other untoward mental states, to assume that these were symptoms of long-standing mental illness mistakenly ascribed to demonic possession, is to assume that they were similarly afflicted at the time of their detention and to ignore the effects of years of mental and physical torture. That they survived such sustained ordeal may, in fact, suggest that this pioneer sample of the mentally ill represented the psychologically sturdiest of the population-at-large.

If the term *psychotic* has any meaning, not as medicine, but as metaphor for, let us say, "outrageously warped behavior," surely it was the messianic, delusional, sadistic, and sexually twisted inquisitors, rather than their victims, who warranted the labels. But though the psychiatric interpretation is grossly incongruent with reality, it is totally congruent with the explanation of the historical relationship of psychiatrist and inquisitor put forth by Szasz: that the mental-illness movement came to *replace* the witchcraft movement, using more benevolent but similar tactics, based on similar concepts, for similar purposes.

PARALLELS OF DEMONOLOGY
AND PSYCHIATRY

The balance of Szasz's argument is based largely on similarities between the movements. These are summarized below, with some additional data and commentary of my own.

The Law

There were two kinds of law in the Middle Ages: secular law, which dealt with crimes against the state, and Divine Law, for crimes against God ("act-crimes" and "thought-crimes" in Szasz's terminology). The judicial procedures of secular law embodied many of the safeguards for civil rights now found in common law: the defendant had the right of counsel, he was tried under fixed rules of evidence, and allowed bail, for example. The accused under Divine Law was automatically divested of all such rights. The church had supreme power.

So today, we have common law and psychiatric law. Whereas common law has grown painfully but progressively more egalitarian, the civil rights of the accused under psychiatric law remain as limited as they were in the inquisitions. In most places in North America, psychiatrists can inter people for at least several days without a court order. The securement of a court order is rarely more than the simplest of formalities, and then the sentence is indeterminate. There are provisions for appeal by patients, usually after a month or so, but appeal boards generally comprise, in part, other psychiatrists, who form an even more cohesive group than physicians proper, and the lay members would naturally tend to defer to the judgments of the medical professionals. Moreover, it is extremely difficult to show that you are sane when you've been professionally labelled as not, and nigh impossible after the wear and tear of a reluctant month or more in a mental institution.

What proportion of institutionalized patients are involuntary? In any veridical sense of the word, 100 percent. Fewer than this *enter* hospitals involuntarily – the actual figure is uncertain, but Szasz estimated 90 percent in 1970[3] and others have repeated this statistic – but all state and provincial laws of which I am aware provide instantaneous mechanisms for converting a resident mental patient's status from voluntary to involuntary, usually the signature of one psychiatrist. And, in my experience, many patients agree to voluntary admission under the threat that they will otherwise be committed, and thus will find it harder to obtain release.

The rationale of the psychiatric inquisitor is basically the same as that of his ecclesiastical predecessor. Victims are deprived of their freedom and civil liberties for their own good; for the redemption of their souls in the earlier era, for their minds in the present. Why can't the victims take the same responsibilities as everyone else for their souls or minds? Because they are not responsible. They have lost control of their judgmental powers to some external invader with whom the inquisitor must do battle: the devil of witchcraft or the virus of mental illness.

Confessions

Most of those accused of witchcraft were condemned by their own confessions, which were extracted by protracted torture or the threat of such. Confessed witches were imprisoned for life or strangled to death. Those who did not confess were deemed "unrepentant," the most serious of charges, and were usually burned alive.

The modern form of the confession is more subtle, but not much more so. It is an axiom of psychiatry that the first, essential step in remediation of mental illness is acceptance by the patient of his condition. Though most people assume that physicians do not make pronouncements of serious disease without strong evidence, many mental patients remain openly skeptical of their clinical labels, aware, perhaps, that the diagnosis was not bestowed on the basis of a physical examination of any kind.

Confessed mental patients tend to have relatively benign encounters with the system, usually a few foggy weeks of institutional infantilization. The unrepentant, however, have a much harder time. Every day that they continue to deny their affliction adds progressively longer increments to their sentences. Deemed more seriously ill than those confessing, they are allowed less freedom of mobility and activity, and attempts to avoid or resist treatment are met by furious retaliation, which may take the form of injections that leave them stuporous for two or three days, or the ultimate devices for rendering mental patients "amenable": shock therapy or psychosurgery.

Witches Teats and Rorschach Signs

Inquisitors of old sometimes employed objective tests of demonic possession, the foremost of which was to search the body for any unique mark that could represent the brand of the devil, for example, inverted nipples, which have come to be called, colloquially, "witches teats." Much attention was focussed on the genital area in these searches. Contemporary inquisitors sometimes use objective tests, as well, which may for example, require their patients to construct images from inkblots, or make up stories, or draw pictures. Much attention is focussed on direct or implied sexual content in these markings.

One could fill a fair-sized closet with the available research reports on the validity of clinical psychological tests, validity meaning the accuracy of tests in identifying individuals who have been judged by other criteria to be mentally ill, or in discriminating among patients considered to have different types of mental illness. The results are, at most, just slightly better than the results that would have been found for witches teats, if appropriate empirical procedures had been in use then.[4] This fact has not stanched the use of these tests, however. The general response by clinicians to the validation data is that test results, nevertheless, are informative "if used in conjunction with other information by a skilled examiner."

I have always been puzzled about what kinds of skills, short of black magic, enable one to generate valid information from invalid measures. The clinicians I have asked have usually told me that they use test items informally; that is, they might employ several pictures of the Thematic Apperception Test to elicit stories but they interpret these in a subjective and qualitative, rather than the prescribed quantitative manner, and assimilate their interpretations with everything else they know about the examinee.

I have two quibbles with this response:

• A minor one, which is mainly semantic, is that the essence of testing is standardization and quantification. It is meaningless and misleading to regard conclusions from the informal, idiosyncratic use of items as "test results." In the example given, pictures from the daily newspaper could have served as well as those from the Thematic Apperception Test.

• The major quibble is that it is mostly a lie. Confront a clinician about the lack of validity of standardized tests and he will tell you about informal, nonquantitative uses. Scrutinize the diagnostic reports he sends to agencies and they are replete with scores, subscores, graphic profiles, and percentiles. Agencies would probably be loath to pay steep professional fees for conclusions based on idiosyncratic applications of invalid measures. And, as one clinician put it in a moment of guilelessness, "Before you say someone is dangerous and lock him up, you have to have concrete reasons . . . so we use test results."

Further, it is apparent that virtually no one was found innocent by the test of skin blemishes, just as virtually no one is found mentally healthy by clinical psychological tests. Rickey Miller, when she was a student of mine in 1974, interviewed 27 psychodiagnosticians in psychiatric hospitals and wards.[5] Among her questions about their selections and uses of tests, she asked, at my behest, whether their conclusions ever showed a person to be free of mental illness. Twelve replied in the affirmative. The comments of some of the others follow.

> To test a person at a point in time and say he's normal is unrealistic . . . everyone is abnormal in some way.

> A test like the Rorschach is designed to measure pathology. How could a patient come out healthy on that one?

> Mine is an analytic approach. I feel everyone has defense mechanisms which inhibit self-actualization.

> Since everyone can benefit from treatment I have never encountered a person who was shown not to need treatment.

> If I can't find anything else wrong with the person, I assume he's psychopathic.

To the twelve who replied positively, Rickey followed the question with a request to see an example of a test protocol which showed no symptoms of mental illness, with the patients' names concealed, if they wished. Some refused outright, others terminated the interview at that point, and still others searched through their files, but no protocols were produced.

Conceptual Flexibility

In order for the inquisitions to fulfill their ideological purposes for some 500 years, definitions of witchcraft had to be sufficiently flexible to conform to different social and theological aims in different times and places. Descriptions of psychiatric categories and symptoms have been similarly adaptable. Thus, *drapetomania*, the mental disease that supposedly caused black slaves in the United States to abscond to freedom, disappeared suddenly with the Reconstruction. *Masturbatory insanity* waned more slowly, as social attitudes toward the practice gradually became less negative over the past 100 years. The diagnosis changed from psychosis to neurosis to mild perversion, then the view prevailed that the only unhealthy aspect was feeling guilty about it. Currently, many psychiatrist and psychologist sex therapists teach masturbation techniques to patients.

The most dramatic eradication of illness occurred in the early 1970s when the American Psychological Association, followed by the American Psychiatric Association, struck *homosexuality* from their lists of mental disorders. There were no scientific discoveries underlying these actions, but the gay-liberation movement was having an increasing effect on public attitudes and legislation.

The adaptibility of psychiatric definitions to social change is nowhere more apparent than in the recent procedures for revision of the *Diagnostic and Statistical Manual of Mental Disorders* (2nd edition).[6] Rather than a panel of acknowledged experts, quietly assimilating the scientific advances of the recent past, it was a public exercise within the field, responsive to social and political interests of all kinds. Thus, from one description of the process:

> . . . a veteran's group successfully lobbied for a syndrome they wanted to call "Post-Vietnam Combat Disorder." Feminist women forced a change in a category called "Sexual Sadism," which they argued would excuse rapists from responsibility for their acts.[7]

In the end, the entire membership of the American Psychiatric Association voted on the Manual, a procedure similar to ratifying a political party platform.

The Victims

The great majority of involuntarily institutionalized mental patients are, as were the victims of the inquisitions, lower socioeconomic, poorly educated people. Just as this discrepancy caused no embarrassment to the theory of witchcraft – it was assumed that those favored by title and holdings were favored in the eyes of God and less susceptible to the Devil – the theories of psychiatry maintain that upper classes tend to be insulated from serious mental illness, for example, by virtue of superior genetic endowment or nutrition.[8]

THE TRANSITION: MORAL AND MENTAL WEAKNESS

Texts tend to gloss over the 200-year transitional period between witchcraft and mental illness. For the revelations about this significant chapter in psychiatry's development, we are indebted mainly to Michael Foucault,[9] although included in the discussion that follows are several archival sources collected by Szasz.[10]

With the close of the Thirty Years' War in 1648, the uneasy partnership in power of church and nobility was severed throughout most of Europe. Gone were the inquisitors and their chambers of death and torture. But gone, as well, were their services as agents of social control, for, along with heretics and wayward women, these chambers were convenient dumping grounds for nuisance populations: vagrants, petty criminals, the feebleminded, incipient revolutionaries. So the dungeons of the inquisitions were rapidly replaced by secular houses of confinement, called hospitals, asylums, retreats, and the like, which were the direct forerunners of contemporary mental institutions. The landmark was the Hospital General of Paris which, shortly after its opening in 1656, housed one percent of the populace of that city. By the last quarter of the seventeenth century, counterparts existed in every major city in France and similar institutions for involuntary incarceration permeated the Continent and had begun to spread throughout the American colonies.

The victim's label changed from witch to patient, and so did the rationale for detention. People were no longer confined to be purged of demons, but of "mental and moral weakness," which at that time were overtly, rather than covertly, regarded as synonymous. The nature of the victim population changed somewhat. Innovations of mass production created a vast class of unemployed throughout Europe, most of whom became petty thieves and street beggars, and as much anathemas to secular authorities as heretics were to their clerical forebears. Thus, the Royal Edict establishing the Hospital General described "mendicancy and idleness" as "the source of all disorders." [11] Needless to say, the main target group remained the poor and uneducated, though the wanton persecution of women of any class was also as prevalent as in the past. Szasz discovered the following piece by English journalist and novelist Daniel Defoe, written in 1728:

This leads me to exclaim against the vile practice now so much in vogue amongst the better Sort, as they are called, but the worst sort, in fact, namely of sending their wives to Mad-Houses at every Whim or Dislike . . . If they are not mad when they go into these cursed houses, they are soon made so by the barbarous Usage they there suffer . . . suddenly clap'd up, stipp'd whipp'd, ill fed, and worse us'd. [12]

As Defoe's passage suggests, physical abuse remained the order of the day under the new oppressors. The genocide and routine, extreme tortures of the inquisition abated, but the Royal Edict stated that the directors of the Hospital General, to keep order, shall have "stakes, irons, prisons and dungeons . . . as much as they deem necessary." [13]

Psychiatry, in its nascent form, was always a partner in the enterprise, though a minor partner initially: the first directors of the Hospital General employed one physician for all three of its domiciles. Gradually, but tenaciously, psychiatry increased its domain. In Florence, in 1774, a decree by the Grand Duke ordered a "mental examination" prior to all internments, thereby initiating the rite of the medical certificate. In 1793, psychiatrist Phillipe Pinel became the first director of the Hospital General from the field of medicine. The next century witnessed psychiatrists in their foremost role: as ideologists of the new inquisition. In all lands they descended upon the houses of confinement, observing, testing, experimenting, classifying, searching for common medical denominators among the variform social and economic unfortunates imprisoned there. In this era and setting were spawned our major current classifications and descriptions of mental illness. The juxtaposition in time and place of the beginning of the era with the French Revolution may suggest that the professed new social and political climate of egalitarianism required a more substantial justification than mendicancy and idleness for the isolation of surplus populations.

"AN ERECT POSITION OF THE BODY," AND OTHER MEDICAL REFORMS

Historians of psychiatry regard Phillipe Pinel as the undisputed founder of the modern field, and the originator of great humanitarian reform. A classic painting of him overseeing the removal of chains from patients is a standard entry in psychiatric and psychological texts. Two of Pinel's own descriptions of his "moral treatment," however, both recovered from the archives by Szasz, reveal that it was but a slightly subtler shade of physical and mental persecution. One program, cited for its therapeutic success,

> . . . consisted of giving full employment to the remaining faculties of the lunatic . . . Some were employed as beasts of draught or burden, and others as servants of various orders and provinces. Fear was the operative principle that gave motion and harmony to this rude system. Disobedience and revolt, whenever they appeared in any of its operations, were instantly and severely punished.

> [In another program of which he approved,] one of the inspectors visited each chamber, at least once every day. If he found any of the manics behaving extravagantly, stirring up quarrels or tumults, making objections to his victuals, or refusing to go to bed at night, he was told in a manner, which of itself was calculated to terrify him, that unless he instantly conformed, he

would have to receive in the morning ten severe lashes as a punishment for his disobedience. The threat was invariably executed with the greatest punctuality. . . .[14]

On the other side of the Atlantic, Benjamin Rush, whose portrait as the father of American Psychiatry is enshrined on the official seal of the American Psychiatric Association, presented his own version of "moral treatment" shortly after Pinel. His therapeutic recommendations included: immersion in cold water; food deprivation; purgatives, emetics, and blood-letting; solitude and darkness; suspension and rapid rotation of the patient, strapped in a chair, in midair; and, "an erect position of the body," which he described as follows:

> There is a method of taming refractory horses in England, by first impounding them, as it is called, and then keeping them from lying down or sleeping, by thrusting sharp pointed nails into their bodies for two or three days and nights. The same advantages, I have no doubt, might be derived from keeping madmen in a standing posture, and awake, for four and twenty hours, but by different and more lenient means.[15]

The final chapter of the second great inquisition remains to be written. Mental institutions retain, as a primary social function, the disposition and control of potentially bothersome surplus populations created by economic change. Sociologist Harvey Brenner, in 1973, showed that the most potent predictor of variations in mental hospitalization rates in New York State over the previous 127 years was unemployment rates.[16] The impoverished, uneducated, and otherwise socially and economically powerless still compose the prime target group.

The rights of the confined have not meaningfully changed since the provisions of the Royal Edict of the Hospital General that, ". . . no appeal will be accepted from the regulations they [the doctors] establish within the said hospital." [17] The mental hospital is still the sole medical entity wherein treatment, of any nature and duration, is mandatory. And the spirit of Pinel and Rush is alive and flourishing within its walls. It takes the form of standardized barbarities rationalized as "treatments," such as psychosurgery, shock therapies, forced administrations of stupor-inducing drugs, and "quiet rooms" for solitary confinement, as well as those abuses of an informal sort: beatings, sexual abuses, deprivation, and humiliations, widespread and well documented in every generation through to the present.[18]

Psychiatry now stands in a nearly exact relationship to the state as the church of the Middle Ages was to the Reformation; only nearly exact because the mental-health professions are not full partners in power with the state, but mere instruments of social, legislative, and judicial agencies. But if this offers some redemption to the professions, it is nevertheless so that they persevered to gain and hold this position. The following chapter explores their major effort in this behalf.

A LABEL IN PURSUIT OF
A DISEASE:
Schizophrenia from Kraepelin to D.S.M. III

Seekers of idols generally turn up something. The great psychiatric quest of the nineteenth century yielded *schizophrenia.*

For the invention (one would be hard pressed to call it a discovery) we are indebted to psychiatrist Emil Kraepelin, though he named it *dementia praecox,* loosely translated from the Latin as "premature mental deterioration." Kraepelin's treatise on dementia praecox comprised a compendium of behaviors ascribed to the disease of such range and diversity as to defy summary. Included were hallucinations, delusions, and all manner of seemingly irrational behaviors associated with madness through the ages, interspersed with descriptions of acts and traits that might be regarded, at the most, as mildly inappropriate. Often, the "symptoms" were mutually contradictory. To cite some examples: [1]

• Patients are "unattentive," he tells us, "their thoughts frequently wander" (p. 6). But on the same page we find that, "The attention is often rigidly fixed. They do not let themselves be interrupted in some definite piece of work."

• In one place we read, "The singular indifference of the patients toward their former emotional relations . . . is not seldom the first and most striking symptom" (p. 33). In another, ". . . senseless jealousy is not rare. His wife has secretly married another man; the nurse wishes to alienate the loved one" (p. 36). And in a third, ". . . there sometimes takes place in the patients a complete reversal of their emotional relationships, which may be first sign of the approaching illness. Former feelings of affection are changed into downright aversion" (p. 36).

• We are told that patients become "shy of their fellow being, withdraw themselves, shut themselves up, do not greet their friends anymore," (p. 96), but elsewhere we find that they, "conduct themselves in a free and easy way . . . speak familiarly to strangers, decorate themselves with gay ribbons" (p. 34).

• Patients "do not follow what happens in their surroundings," "betray neither by look nor by demeanor in any way that they are sensitive to external impressions," (p. 6) but they sometimes show a "distinct inquisitiveness . . . surreptitiously watch what happens in the room, follow the physician at a distance, look in at all open doors" (p. 7).

• We learn that "the patients have lost every independent inclination for work and action; they sit about idle . . . experience no tediousness, have no need to pass the time" (p. 37). They are often found, however, to "busy themselves with trifling affairs, make wreaths of flowers, exert themselves to learn poems off by heart, or to begin Latin" (p. 97).

• In matters sexual, the disease manifests itself by "the want of a feeling of shame" (p. 34). Female patients, though, are concerned, "that men wish to seduce them . . . that they have lost their virtue, that their honor has been tarnished" (p. 30).

• Patients suffer a "weakening of volitional impulses . . . which specially give the clinical picture its peculiar stamp." Lost is the "activity of the will . . . the resistance which outside influences meet within us. The patients, therefore are usually docile, let themselves be driven as a herd" (p. 37). On the other hand, we are apprised of the symptom of "negativism . . . the unapproachable, repellant behavior of the patients. . . . They do not return a greeting . . . draw back when one approaches them . . . resist obstinately every regulation" (p. 108). "Often the patients refuse [to give the physician] all information [saying], 'That is their own affair,' 'That is no one's business.' . . . A patient first asked the physician to show him his diplomas that he might know with whom he had to do. Others give perverted or quite insufficient answers" (p. 49).

Kraepelin's contribution, then, was a diagnostic label that could be applied to virtually any behavior, irrational or otherwise; a more exotic but no more informative concept than "moral and mental weakness." Nowhere do we learn what proportion of patients showed what specific behaviors of patterns. Were there 2 percent who reported hallucinations compared to 92 percent who merely "conducted themselves in a free and easy way?" We are told, instead, that the "fundamental disturbances," that is, of attention, thought, and conduct, "cannot for the most part be regarded as characteristic," because they take "the most diverse combinations" (p. 5). There was an attempt to develop subclassifications of the disease, called "clinical forms," but the introduction to this section cautions that:

The presentation of clinical details in the large domain of dementia praecox meets with considerable difficulties, because a delimitation of the different clinical pictures can only be accomplished artificially. There is certainly a whole series of phases which frequently return, but between them there are such numerous transitions that in spite of all efforts it appears impossible at present to delimit them sharply and to assign each case without objection to a definite form.[2]

The ambiguity of this passage seems more befitting a political than a scientific treatise, but if Kraepelin was saying that he *tried* to develop diagnostic subcategories, based on homogeneous patterns of symptoms, and failed, then history has certainly borne him out.

In one respect was Kraepelin firm: that patients rarely improved, almost always "deteriorated" further. He was not clear at all about the precise progression, offering another collection of unquantified and divergent illustrations. Further, never was the possibility explored or even suggested that such decomposition, in whatever forms it occurred, represented the explicable consequences of years of inhumane confinement, degradation, and brutalization.

In any case, this was the only aspect of Kraepelin's description that irked the sensibilities of his psychiatric colleagues, and the renaming of the disease, to *schizophrenia* (from the Greek, "splitting of the mind"), by Eugene Bleuler in 1911, was based almost entirely on this digression.[3] Why the obsession with this one particular conjecture, Kraepelin's most precise and coherent, so early in the game? Could it be that it did not suit the ambitions of the

field? *The Comprehensive Textbook of Psychiatry*, in seeming innocence, states that the notion of progressive deterioration was re-
jected because it made it "rather awkward" for the clinician, who
was thereby unable to both confirm his diagnosis without waiting
several years and "pursue his therapeutic task constructively." [4]
In the magic of psychiatry, whatever is inconvenient may be
altered by the sweep of a pen.

The new term signified, in Bleuler's definition, a loss of "unity"
in the persons' mental function,[5] but there were virtually no limits
to the way in which this disunity could be expressed; for example,
wandering attention, inappropriate emotional expression, idiosyncratic verbal communication. Thus, the entire range of Kraepelin's
descriptions, and more, were subsumed under the new label.

THE MODERN CONCEPT

Today, schizophrenia is the most intimidating word in
psychiatry's arsenal of jargon, providing the field with most of its
aura of mystery and complexity and more than half of its hospital
patients. Definitions and diagnostic criteria, however, have
become no more precise in nearly a century. On a broad geographical scale, they seem to reflect local social custom. Thus, your
chances of being diagnosed schizophrenic are four times greater in
Western Ireland than in the United States; two and one-half times
greater if you live in New England than in the midwest; signifi-
cantly higher in the upper than in the lower socioeconomic classes
in India, but this is reversed in the United States, England, and
Japan.[6] Studies in which pairs of psychiatrists independently
assessed the same individuals have shown rates of agreement on
the diagnosis as low as 53 percent,[7] which, given that about 50
percent of mental patients are called schizophrenic, represents
pure chance. Finally, from the research and cases we have examined, it is apparent that very ordinary people can earn and keep
the label merely by finding themselves in an appropriate context.

All of which is cheerfully acknowledged by the profession. The
Comprehensive Textbook of Psychiatry maintains that "diagnosis
remains the greatest impediment to investigative work in schizophrenia" and, though it is generally held that schizophrenia is
easier to detect in long-term patients than those in the initial

stages, "reliable diagnostic criteria have not been established for either patient category." [8] Another contemporary source book informs us that, regarding schizophrenia, "such is the symptomatic variety seen today that our presently held diagnostic categories are inadequate to describe them," [9] and a third states: "The odds against writing anything sensible, informed and useful about the diagnosis of schizophrenia are tremendous." [10]

Then how is it done?

DIAGNOSING SCHIZOPHRENIA: TEXTBOOK VERSIONS

Textbooks tend to be fairly homogeneous in their descriptions of the symptoms of schizophrenia, and most include those listed below, which have descended virtually intact from Bleuler. Most also separate symptoms, as did Bleuler, in terms of "fundamental", the first seven of the list, and "accessory", the last two. Fundamental symptoms are always present to some degree, which means anything from one to all of the seven are present, and they may manifest one time, occasionally, or continuously. Accessory symptoms are more rarely seen.

1. *Looseness of associations:* A lack of apparent purposiveness of communication, that is, lack of movement toward a logical point.
2. *Flight of ideas:* Moving rapidly from one thought to another in communication, without customary pauses or other signals of demarcation.
3. *Thought blocking:* Abrupt lapses or cessations of conversation.
4. *Inappropriate affect:* Emotional expression unsuited to the situation.
5. *Ambivalence:* Conflicted feelings and responses.
6. *Attentional deficit:* A lack of attention to the immediate surroundings.
7. *Autism:* A withdrawal into the self, a preoccupation with wishes, desires, fantasies.
8. *Delusions:* Misinterpretations of reality.
9. *Hallucinations:* Bodily sensations without apparent cause.

Textbooks are also very similar in their illustrations of schizophrenic symptoms. For looseness of associations and flight of ideas, there are invariably excerpts from letters or conversations such as:

Am I a good cook? It depends on whose house I'm cooking. . . .
No I haven't had any dreams. They took the Ladies Home Journal out of my room. . . .

The players and boundaries have been of different colors in
terms of black and white and I do not intend that the futuramas
of supersonic fixtures will ever be in my life again. . . .[11]

Examples of inappropriate affect generally include the inces-
sant giggling of the so-called *hebephrenic* type of schizophrenia, or
patients who smile broadly while telling some tale of great woe or
who adopt an attitude of total indifference to whatever happens
around them.

The classic example of both attentional deficit and autism is
the catatonic type, who remains largely mute and immobile for
days or weeks or longer. Sometimes cited, as well, are patients
who carry on animated conversations with no one present or who
act out egocentric impulses in public, such as singing loudly during
a concert.

Illustrative delusions are either grandiose or persecutory in
nature, both regarded as symptoms of the paranoid type. The patient is Jesus Christ or the President (Napoleon seems to have
fallen out of vogue), or he believes some espionage organization is
pursuing him, or he speaks of a large fortune he has secreted
somewhere.

Examples of hallucinations generally involve voices arguing,
demanding, or admonishing. Sometimes, as well, there are visual
or tactile illustrations; bright lights under the eyelids or snakes
writhing in the stomach.

The paradox may be becoming evident: if all, or most schizophrenics actually behaved in the grossly atypical ways depicted in
textbooks, there would be virtually no problem of identification.
We might quarrel about what it was that was being diagnosed, but
there would be little question about who had it and who didn't.
Regional discrepancies and differences of opinion between examiners would represent rare events rather than rules. The Temberlin and the Rosenhan studies could not have happened, nor could
the various cases we described. It would be very difficult to invoke
the diagnosis to confine someone for reasons other than bizarre
behavior. Psychiatric and psychological texts would not bemoan
the lack of reliable diagnostic criteria.

The resolution of the paradox is that most people termed schizophrenic do not behave in any manner remotely resembling text-book cases. They are, instead, like the people I've described in my seminar-in-a-madhouse, all of whom, in fact, were diagnosed schizophrenic. Then, how do they qualify?

DIAGNOSING SCHIZOPHRENIA: WHAT REALLY HAPPENS

If the reader would return to the descriptions of symptoms, ignoring the illustrative material for the moment, he will note that, even as a system for categorizing grossly atypical behavior, it is remarkably crude. The terms, for the most part, harbor highly ambiguous referents, and, thus, much potential for overlap and confusion. Is a person who seems indifferent to everything around him showing attentional deficit, inappropriate affect, or autism? Is thought blocking an expression of ambivalence? When does flight of ideas become looseness of associations?

Why, in all of this time, have we not striven for more refinement and coherence? It is because the crudity of the system suits it admirably to its actual use, as a set of categories which can be applied, more or less, to anyone in any situation, and, more rather than less, to persons undergoing crises which would lead to contact with the mental-health professions, or simply responding to the stresses and ambiguities of a psychiatric interview, involuntarily or otherwise.

Thus, looseness of associations, flight of ideas, and thought blocking, in the broader application, refer to anything less than total clarity of communication, an affliction I am certain all of us have suffered at one time or another, or perceived in others, particularly at times of turmoil, or anger, or when attempting to give verbal expression to vague, suppressed emotions.

Consider the following excerpt I recorded at the intake interview of a woman who had been escorted to a mental hospital following a tumultuous emotional outburst during a family quarrel:

It all comes tumbling in from all sides. Everybody wants a piece of me . . . just a piece. My husband is a sonofabitch. I wish I didn't need so much. Do you really give a damn, doctor? These goddamned walls . . . These goddamned white walls. I'm always

inside white walls. White walls in my head . . . come crashing
down and it all comes tumbling in. Doctor, you don't really give
a damn. None of you do.

No more esoteric than the rambling, allegorical discourse of a
very distraught person; but sufficient for a diagnosis of schizophrenia based on loose associations and its cousin, flight of ideas.
Had she tried to contain her emotions and, perhaps, answered the
psychiatrist's probing questions hesitantly, incompletely, then she
would have been committed on thought blocking.

Inappropriate affect is another catchall. What, after all, is an
appropriate affect for a psychiatric examination, particularly one
that is involuntary? Many interviewees, in response to the oppression of the situation itself, or whatever events brought them there,
become sullen, distant, withdrawn, uncommunicative. Others
react defensively: attempt to be glib and humorous, perhaps to
show their disdain for the interviewer or to discredit the allegation
of their insanity. In either case, they lose to inappropriate affect.

Ambivalence and attentional deficit, in the benign as opposed
to bizarre forms, hardly require explication. Howard, in my
seminar-in-a-madhouse, earned his schizophrenic label on the basis
of his ambivalences toward his dependency on his mother and his
job. Attentional deficit often means that the subject tuned the interviewer out at some point.

The concept of autism may pertain to any aspect of a person's
fantasy life. The following response by a male during an interview
I attended was interpreted, not atypically, as a sign of autism suggesting schizophrenia:

> I live my life in daydreams too much. I'm always some kind of
> hero . . . a secret agent or a famous athlete. Even in my sex
> life . . . I imagine that I'm some kind of very masculine heroic
> figure when I'm making love.

The autism category is used most frequently in the diagnosis
of *childhood schizophrenia,* and while there are children who fit
the textbook descriptions of constant, almost total withdrawal
into fantasy, I have seen the term applied to children who were
simply shy and avoided initiating friendships, or who tended to
daydream during classroom hours.

Even if the examinee manages to elude all of these traps, though it is difficult to conceive how, there is the supreme Catch 22: "lack of insight," defined as the inability to recognize the nature and consequences of one's own behavior. For whatever reasons, it is rarely included in texts as a sign of schizophrenia, but in my own observations, and in one large-scale survey,[12] it appears more frequently than any other in diagnostic reports. To be judged as suffering lack of insight, you need merely disagree with your psychiatric examiner that your behavior is indicative of mental illness. Thus, if you admit that you are ill and in need of treatment, then you are obviously ill and in need of treatment. If you deny that you are ill and in need of treatment, then you are even more obviously ill and in need of treatment.

It may seem that benign forms of delusions and hallucinations would be more difficult to come by, and, perhaps this is why they are relegated to the status of accessory symptoms.

Delusions, however, need not be outrageously fanciful. Disagreements with the examiner about the motives and intents of others will qualify. Frank, in my seminar-in-a-madhouse was adjudged paranoid schizophrenic on the basis of his claim that the police had persecuted him, and I have seen many others regarded as delusional based on plausible, or at least comprehensible, assertions about the ill intent of their families or the hospital staff toward them.

Exaggerations or outright lies qualify, as well. One impoverished patient's delusion of grandeur consisted of telling the interviewer he had at one time amassed a great deal of money through investments. One middle-aged man, with a grade school education, was so delusional as to maintain that he was going to become a psychiatrist someday.

Allegorical descriptions, particularly in the area of religiosity, though acceptable and even esteemed in many circles outside the mental hospital, readily become delusions inside. One teenaged girl, brought to the hospital by her father who objected, among other things, to her intention to join a demonstration against environmental pollution, told her examiner that she felt it was her "mission from God," and thereby became a paranoid schizophrenic. An elderly woman had been twice hospitalized as paranoid schizophrenic, based on her statements that she had been "taken over by the devil." My questioning revealed that her devil had no form or substance, but that she was a devout fundamentalist who regarded all of her moral conflicts as battles within herself between the forces of Heaven and Hell.

Figurative speech is not infrequently interpreted as hallucination, as well. Two extreme instances come to mind, both from reports by psychiatrists who were apparently unacquainted with Western colloquialisms. The "clear hallucination" of one of these patients was that she claimed "her nerves got in the way" on job interviews. The other said, in response to the question of how she felt, that she had "butterflies in her stomach," which was entered in her diagnostic report as "hallucinating insects in her abdomen." Cultural misunderstandings aside, I have also seen cast as hallucination such mundane descriptions of bodily sensations as: "feels pressure in his head whenever he is tense"; "feels lightheaded occasionally, as if he could float"; "says that her skin tightens when she is upset."

One can ascertain indirectly, but with fair accuracy, from the diagnostic report whether a patient labelled schizophrenic showed gross atypical behavior of any kind. These, particularly in the sections dealing with "mental status," tend to be very tersely stated, composed of unqualified abstractions such as: "paranoid ideation," "loose associations," "constricted thought," "mood swings," "impaired judgment." Occasionally, however, one finds graphic detail; for example, "The patient claimed he was the reincarnation of Christ and that God spoke to him through the radio," or, "She communicated in a disconnected series of associations, saying, at one point, that she was a close friend of the President and, immediately afterward, that all the doctors in the hospital had tried to seduce her." What I have found is that when examiners observe the bizarre, they tend to describe it in glorious detail, and when there was no such description, there was no such behavior.

My perusal of hundreds of schizophrenic diagnostic reports from various locales revealed about 10 percent with precise descriptions of aberrance. This figure is congruent with my own direct observations and with those of several of my colleagues, who spent their careers in mental hospitals, of the approximate proportion of diagnosed schizophrenics who behave in an unequivocally bizarre manner. It is also the estimate found by Foucault of the proportion of incarcerations in the Hospital General of Paris that involved persons who were "insane or demented."[13] Thus, the descent from demonic possession through moral and mental weakness to schizophrenia appears totally consistent, untrammeled, at any stage, by science, medicine, or truth. The labels have changed in response to changing sociocultural orientations, but have remained sufficiently ambiguous and flexible to encompass any and all individuals who, in the eyes of arbiters of social custom, warranted isolation and confinement, including, in small minority, those we might regard as mad.

It should now be abundantly clear why diagnosticians cannot agree on individual cases, why incidence rates for schizophrenia vary so across social classes and geographic areas, how perfectly sound individuals, whether part of an experiment or not, can be placed, so readily, in the category. The most instrumental, and often the sole, factor in the diagnosis of schizophrenia is whether the examiner wishes to bestow it. No one who comes in contact with the psychiatric establishment can, by his own devices, avoid the label. One of the most compelling classroom demonstrations I do is a mock psychiatric interview with a volunteer class member, with the others noting all of the schizophrenic signs he evidences. It usually evolves into group hilarity but, in life, it is not at all amusing.

THE REFORMATION OF 1980

Some of this may finally have permeated the establishment, though, more likely, they are simply becoming increasingly defensive in response to increasing revelations of their capriciousness. The 1980 revised edition of the *Diagnostic and Statistical Manual* appears to attempt a more stringent definition of schizophrenia, but on closer examination, this is more apparent than real:
• First, it is stressed in several places that schizophrenia entails "overt psychotic features." Definitions of *psychotic* actually vary considerably themselves, but usually pertain in some respect to a lack of contact with "reality." The Manual's glossary defines it as, "gross impairment of reality testing." [14]

This emphasis on psychotic features is a most revealing redundancy inasmuch as schizophrenia has always been classified as a psychosis and regarded as the most serious. Psychiatrists, as we have noted, keep the schizophrenic rosters filled by means of their frivolous interpretations of reality: allegories become loose associations, resentments become paranoid delusions, social withdrawal becomes autism.

• Second, there is a provision that the patient showed "deterioration from a previous level of functioning." [15] This seems to be an attempt to get closer to the model of medicine proper. If someone weighs 140 pounds all of his adult life, it has a different connotation than if he suddenly dropped from 180 to 140. But if someone informs a psychiatrist that he hears angels whispering in his ear, and he has all of his life, shall he then be pronounced healthy?

Of course, in practice, virtually everyone who comes into contact with the mental health profession has undergone some change, whether in his own eyes or in the eyes of others, so we can safely assume that the qualification will not impose any real limits on the diagnostician.

• The third innovation is the oddest of all, especially in light of the second. It states, "The diagnosis is not made unless the period of illness has persisted for at least six months." [16] Could this be a return to the Kraepelinian concept of inevitable deterioration? And whence came the magic number of six months? Was it by caucus and negotiation between those who would like to have less schizophrenia and those who would not?

Again, the prospect of this qualification put to practice seems baffling, particularly since it is "the illness" which must persist for six months and not any specific one or more of the variety of alternative behaviors by which it is defined. Will psychiatrists turn away someone who has hoisted himself, Christ-like, on a stake for five and one-half months, and give his place in the hospital to someone else who has been ambivalent for six and one-half?

The crude intent of the six-month rule seems evident: to exclude from the schizophrenic rolls those who have a stray emotional outburst of some sort and find themselves before a mental-health professional. But examiners, if they pay any attention to the rule at all, will probably merely ascertain that the subject did have another outburst or showed some other of the myriad behaviors interpretable as schizophrenia more than six months ago, and business will proceed as usual.

Of course, these prognostications may be unduly pessimistic and psychiatrists may, in fact, attempt to follow the proscriptions of DSM III in letter and spirit. If so, there should be an immediate decline of roughly 90 percent, by our prior analysis, in the incidence of schizophrenia. Those who are sufficiently aberrant to have lost their grasp on reality can be classified schizophrenic under the new standards.

At that time, the concept will be roughly equivalent to madness.

It might appear from the texts that the subcategories of schizophrenia should, at least, provide a system for distinguishing the varieties of madness, but this, too, is illusory. The two most dramatic subtypes: the giggling, slobbering, incontinent hebephrenic; and the mute, immobile, rigidly postured catatonic are virtually nonexistent, a fact that has been publicly acknowledged within the field.[17] Where have they gone? No one ventures to say. The extreme, prolonged withdrawal called "catatonia" may have been an occasional response to the more overtly cruel confinements of an earlier era, and "hebephrenia," which seemed to involve progressive loss of motor control, was probably a real neurological disorder, the source of which was never isolated, and, perhaps, related to some other condition, which has come under hygienic or medical control.

The paranoid type, referring to those expressing delusions of persecution or grandeur, does, in a limited sense, distinguish a particular expression of madness, though no one has ever explained why these two divergent types of delusions should be grouped as one category.

For the most part, patients are cast as *chronic-undifferentiated* types, though the term *acute* is available for those whose madness is more short-lived than others (or those who attempt to stay out of the domain of the mental-health professions after their first encounter) and prepubertal patients are called *childhood type*.

Madness will do just as well.

SEARCHING FOR THE SCHIZOCOCCUS

Of the two million or so people who will be told in the coming year that they suffer from schizophrenia, most will be informed, as well, that it is a disease of biological origin which can be successfully treated by drugs.

How can a mythological disease have a biological origin? It

cannot and it does not. The more astute patient may be impressed with the fact that the diagnosis of his so-called biological condition was not bestowed on the basis of a biological test of any kind. There are none in recognized use, nor have there ever been. Beginning with Kraepelin's reports, a century-long, wide-ranging scrutiny of bodily wastes, fluids, cells, tissues, and organs of people deemed schizophrenic, in vivo and post-mortem, has provided vast numbers of doctoral dissertations and research articles, but not one reliable, biological abnormality associated with the diagnosis.

Nevertheless, psychiatry's perennial claim is that it is on the threshold of a revolution, based on some discovery or other, that is inevitably disconfirmed with more careful research. The following describes a sample of these "breakthroughs"; that is, supposed discoveries of biological correlates of schizophrenia, through recent decades, all heralded for a time and unceremoniously abandoned. The current rage, the dopamine theory, appears to be well on the way to joining the archives.[18]

- *Impaired reactivity:* Lack of response to painful stimuli; abnormal reactions to administrations of sodium amytal, sodium pentathol, phenothiazine, histamine, pitressin, thyroid medication, insulin, adrenalin, mecholyl, dinitorphenol, foreign protein, and pertussis vaccine; lower skin temperature and heat production; lack of thermo-regulatory adaptivity to cold; atypical blood count responses to high humidity; impaired vestibular, galvanic, and pupillary responses.
- *Brain structure:* Swollen nuclei, shrunken neurons, fibrous gliosis; pigmentary changes; lesions of the upper cortical layers and the infracortex of the temporal and parietal lobes; intracytoplasmic inclusions in the neurons; cellular changes in the antroventral and hypothalmic nuclei; increases of lipofuscine and tigrolysis in the pallidum and straitum.
- *Cardiovascular:* Hypoplasia of the cardiovascular and lymphatic systems; degenerative and atrophic changes in the testes; reduced density, wide variability in size, immature formation, and high plexus rating of the capillaries.
- *Endocrinological:* Elevated cerebrospinal fluid protein, abnor-

mal colloidal gold curves; ovarian insufficiencies; menstrual pain, irregularity, and amenorrhea; gross disorders of spermatogenic elements.

- *Hematological:* Dense hemoglobin; reduced resistance of erythrocytes to hemolytic agents; abnormal lymphocytes, leucocytes, protein, and hemolysin; increased reticulum cells in the bone marrow; higher incidence of blood groups A and A_1.
- *Biochemical:* Decreased basal metabolism; defects in the metabolism of carbohydrates, glucose, and lactate; alterations in nitrogen balance; antigenic and immunological abnormalities; increases in 4S and 19S macroglobulins, a-globulin fractions, and the haptoglobin component of blood serum; abnormal amino acid secretion; occurrence of 3, 4-dime-thoxyphenyle-thylamine and indolic compounds in the urine.
- *General:* Pattern dissociations of the fingerprints; functional hypothyroidism; hepatic dysfunction; tubercle baccili in the spinal fluid; neurotropic streptococcal infection; pernicious anemia; abnormal sleeping and waking EEG patterns.[19]

Why does such an exercise in futility continue? Defenders of the enterprise will tell you first about *general paresis*. General paresis was regarded as a mental disorder until 1909, when it was found to be caused by cerebral syphilis. General paresis in 1909; why not schizophrenia in 1989?

What the psychiatric and psychological textbooks usually do not relate, however, is that general paresis was distinguished by a set of homogeneous, neurological symptoms: pupillary abnormalities, speech impediments, tremor, loss of fine and gross motor coordination, and abnormal tendon reflexes, which were regarded as the primary characteristics of the disorder. The search for biological bases for allegorical communication, or social withdrawal, or unrealistic beliefs hardly belongs in the same category of endeavor as the search for a biological basis for general paresis.

Further, advocates of the biological model cite the evidence of a genetic factor in schizophrenia, which is invoked not only to justify the search for biological causes, but to strike proper humility and anxiety into patients and their families who would doubt that there is a real disease at the root of their problem.

THE GENETIC MYTH

The evidence requires careful attention. First, we should be aware that it does not come from the laws of dominant and recessive genes and the Mendelian ratios derived from these, which represent the predominant method for ascertaining genetic determinism. These yield precise probability estimates, from generational histories, for the occurrence of such traits as eye color and such diseases as diabetes.

The evidence for schizophrenia comes from correlational studies: mostly from *co-twin* studies. These are comparisons of concordance rates of the diagnosis between monozygotic (identical) and dizygotic (fraternal) twins. Identical twins have identical inheritance; fraternal twins do not. Thus, higher rates of concordance for the former group – that is, the greater likelihood that either both or neither member of the twin pair will be labeled schizophrenic – is assumed to be attributable to genetic factors.

Unlike Mendelian ratios, co-twin and other correlational studies do not yield probability estimates for occurrence, based on family history; nor do they convey information about the genetic process by which inheritance effects occurrence. Further, by their nature and design, they will reveal statistically significant differences for the most minute, low-level, occasional effects. Thus, less well-publicized co-twin studies have produced similar statistics to schizophrenia for virtually every measurable personality and behavioral characteristic. The following is a partial list:

> Introversion; sociability; shyness; social presence; dominance; dependency needs; needs for affiliation; nervous tension; self-control; impulsivity; personal responsibility; empathy; activity level; aggressiveness; likeableness; self-confidence; vigor; nonconformity; orderliness.[20]

We need look no further than this list for explanations of the correlational, genetic data for schizophrenia that fit all else we have uncovered about the concept. Traits such as non-conformity, introversion, shyness, and dependency are in themselves sufficient to generate the diagnosis, if they provoke sufficient concern of self or of others to bring the person before a mental health professional.

PSYCHIATRIC JUNKIES

Finally, the mental-health professions point to the "chemo-therapy revolution" of the early 1950s: the beginning of the ongoing era of the widespread use of antipsychotic drugs. If schizophrenic behavior can be dispelled by biochemical agents, is it not, then, a biochemical condition?

Of course, two or three martinis or inhalations of marijuana can, for many, dispel inhibitions at a social gathering or worry about day-to-day problems. Shall we then regard social inhibitions and worry as diseases and seek their biological origins? Antipsychotic drugs fall into the same category. Their development was not based on any discoveries about the workings of the brain, nor were they developed for any specific symptom of schizophrenia. They were adapted from general surgery, from antihistaminic derivatives whose stupor-inducing properties were useful in preventing surgical shock. An alert drug company accurately foresaw their enthusiastic reception by psychiatry.

With steady and large enough dosages, patients give up their idiosyncratic discourse, paranoid complaints, excited or depressed behavior, and every other "symptom." These are mind-blunting substances. Ambling about with glazed eyes, shuffling gait, slurred speech, and slowed reflexes, patients need all they can muster to hold mind and body together to get to the bathroom.

Nevertheless, many patients want the drugs and like them. They do often reduce anxiety and agitation, not unlike the standard recreational drugs, but not many of us would seriously consider or recommend perpetual intake of these substances as a means of resolving life's problems.

Many other patients do not want or like the drugs, just as many people in the mainstream do not desire alcohol or marijuana. When recalcitrant patients are forced to take them, as they usually are, they tend to settle into a state of unhappy stupor, just as anyone forced to ingest a recreational drug probably would. Thus, besides helping to justify its biological claims, antipsychotic drugs benefit the mental health establishment in another way: they provide a common denominator, so that no matter how benign or bizarre the patients behaved at the time of their entry into the hospital, all do eventually appear demented. The revised *Diagnos-*

tic and Statistical Manual reminds practitioners, in fact, that "anti-psychotic drugs have effects that may appear similar to the affective blunting and flattening seen in schizophrenia."[21]

Early in my career, a woman whom I had known as a friend and had counselled briefly following her marital breakup, came to tell me she felt unable to cope with job, home, and children, and that she planned to check into a mental hospital for a few days. A week later I learned that she was still there, and I went, unexpected, to visit. Although I had seen this bright, talented woman at the best and worst of her times, I had never seen her in any way like she was that day. Curled up with her head in her arms against the headboard of her bed, her eyes and brain dulled on drugs, it took about five minutes for her to acknowledge my presence and another ten for me to extract from her, in an almost whispered monotone, that she had discovered that she was "very sick . . . had been all her life, with schizophrenia . . . couldn't take care of herself or children . . . had to stay in the hospital for weeks, maybe months. . . ."

More a reflex than anything else, I shook her by her shoulders from her fetal-like crouch and hissed in her face:

> Crap. . . . That's crap. You weren't "very sick" before you came in here . . . you never were . . . you were just very upset. Let's get you the hell out of here so you can be just very upset again, and you can stay with us until we find out what's upsetting you.

A small light broke through the Thorazine haze in her eyes and her voice became a little stronger. "Can I do that?"

"Sure you can. Just get your street clothes on, keep your head up, and no matter what anyone says to you, tell them you want to go. . . . We'll get some pizza on the way home." I saw a thin smile.

We left, but not before I had spent a tense hour cajoling the staff psychiatrist, who wanted to change her status to involuntary because she "seemed so withdrawn." I sat up with her for the better part of a night and a day, watching her come off the drugs and return from "schizophrenic withdrawal" to "just very upset." She stayed at my home and we talked often for about two weeks. The following is some of what she told me of her hospital experience:

> They didn't give me my clothes for three days. The first morning I was "staffed." I sat in a meeting room with three men in

jackets and ties, while I wore a hospital robe that I had to struggle with to keep my backside and frontside covered at the same time. They asked me all kinds of questions but they wouldn't respond to me – not really. One of them wrote in a notebook practically anytime I said anything. Finally I told them that I found the whole thing humiliating and I was sure it was going to make me even more depressed. Two of them just stared and the one with the notebook began to write furiously. Later that day they started giving me drugs. At first I didn't mind them. They mellowed me out a little, but then I wanted to think – get in touch with myself – and the drugs were fogging my mind and making me uncomfortable. But the nurse wouldn't let me stop. She made me open my mouth each time to make sure I swallowed them.

The next day I saw my psychiatrist. She was in her 50's . . . a real tight-ass. . . . She kept asking me about my marriage . . . who did what to who . . . how I felt about my ex-husband . . . other men in my life. I told her that wasn't the issue . . . that wasn't what I couldn't handle. But she wasn't paying me any mind. I asked her if I could get off the medication or take less of it. She shook her head. "You are very, very sick," she said. "You are schizophrenic. You will probably have to take some kind of medication all of your life or you will become much sicker." I didn't have anything more to say to her, so I just slumped down in my chair and shut up. She patted my shoulder and left and I didn't see her again. . . .

My friend had me promise when she left my home that I would come, day or night, if she ever desperately needed me, and that no matter what she said or did, I wouldn't let her near a mental hospital again. She called in my promise just one time, several weeks later. I kept in touch with her for several years afterward and she completed a graduate degree, embarked on a new career, and seemed to have successfully averted the role of "psychiatric junkie."

I have seen many others, however, who did not. Like daytrippers in the park, they all look the same: small, dull smiles; vacuous expressions; tentative, measured responses. They often discard their pills for a while, get in touch with their pains again, return to their doctors, and begin the cycle anew.

IS THERE A BABY IN THE BATHWATER?
On Redeeming the Medical Model

IN DEFENSE OF DUALISM

There are those who speak of redeeming the mental-health professions. Their position is that if the field were divested of its extraneous influences, a renewed and valid psychiatry would emerge. The premise appears to be that if a basically sound concept, like medical science, has been misapplied, the thing to do is to try to reapply it more judiciously.

Biology, however, has been repeatedly misapplied in political ideologies: social Darwinism and *Mein Kampf* are prime examples, but well-intentioned scientists are not engaged in a search for a biologically valid political system. There may be some relationship between the fields; for example, facts about industrial pollution's effects may bear on the question of government regulation in the private sector. In the main, however, biology and politics are best viewed as separate areas of endeavor, suited to separate aspects of the human condition, and attempts to combine them in any global manner inevitably seem prompted by ulterior purpose.

Similarly, medical science has some implications for madness: there are diseases, as we noted in Chapter 2, that lead to aberrant behavior, but any attempt to subsume the study of madness into medical science is bound to be misdirected.

These statements will displease the philosophical purist, for they endorse the heretical doctrine of Cartesian dualism: the separation of mind and body. All that we feel and think and do, it will be pointed out, ultimately is somatically determined. Why not, then, leave the task of unravelling aberrant behavior to the medical scientist? It is one of the prime arguments of the psychiatric revisionist.

I could point out in return that the distinction between inorganic and organic is as much an artificial dichotomy as that between bodies and minds. All, in the end, is reducible to matter and energy. Why not, then, relegate the concerns of medical scientists to microphysicists? Philosophers deal in ultimate truths. Working scientists require categories of convenience in order to make sense of the here and now. Just as biological concepts are the most heuristic for our understanding of bodies even though bodies are ultimately a manifestation of matter, mentalistic concepts are the most heuristic for our understanding of behavior, even though behavior is ultimately a manifestation of biology.

This is, of course, the essence of dualism. Dualists are not oblivious to the nervous system, nor do they deny the unassailable truism that all things ascribed to mind are, in the final analysis, the products of the brain. The point is that as long as this final analysis is not at hand, mind will have to do.

The dualist can also appreciate the fact that certain states of mind, such as anxiety and depression, can be altered by tampering with the nervous system, and that provocative recent advances, such as the theory of the split brain, may generate even more exotic possibilities. Such efforts, however, fascinating as they are, nevertheless do not render forseeable nor even conceivable the time when significant matters of mind can be explained in terms of the brain; when questions about why people become moralists or hedonists, liberals or conservatives, leaders or followers, spiritualists or pragmatists, optimists or pessimists, can be answered in terms of biochemical composition. If that day arrives, it may be productive to search for the medical bases of obscure discourse, distortion of reality, social withdrawal, compulsive ritual, and so forth. On that day, biochemistry will have the final word, as well, about economics, history, literature, art, and all the other activities of humankind. In the meantime, such speculations remain in the realm of science fiction and not science. It is the province of Jeff in my seminar-in-a-madhouse (Chapter 2), who fantasized the day when personalities are created by laser beams, and it is a marvelous irony that psychiatrists put him away while continuing their own inquiries.

Even if Jeff and the psychiatrists could attend the era when science fiction becomes science, they might not be able to appreciate it. The concept of "reflexivity," which refers to "the effect of thinking, feeling and willing on these processes themselves," [1] represents an enigma inherent in a mind attempting to conceive of it's own nature. This enigma may be explained only by an entity of a higher order than man. Can I conceive of a state in which I describe the processes that direct me to write this treatise on mind without invoking concepts of mind? How to think about thinking without thinking?

There are less lofty considerations, however, than the virtues of dualism leading to the conclusion that medical science is ill suited for the study of madness. There are basic assumptions of medical science that are reasonable and functional in their applications to bodies, but that are unreasonable and misleading if applied to behaviors beyond simple reflexes. These premises are *nonvolition* and *nonpurposiveness*.

THE QUESTION OF CONTROL

It is appropriate to talk in terms of nonvolition in regard to somatic ills. We do not choose or control our diseases. We do not grow tumors as we grow house plants or beards. They grow in us. We do not obtain viruses as we do passports or educations. We are afflicted by viruses. We cannot by acts of decision alter these states. Change requires other nonvolitional events within the body or external interventions, called treatments, that function independently of the inclination of the sufferer; that is, they can be administered covertly or forcibly with equal result. (Although there is a viewpoint that volition has more to do with the causes and cures of illness than we believe, this is mainly the outlook of nonmedical healers, and to the extent that it may eventually prevail among physicians, it will require a total theoretical and practical departure from the extant medical model.)

By definition, then, the basic tenet of the medical approach to madness is that the mind of the mad person is *out of its own con-*

trol.[2] This is also the assumption of the mystical approach and, whereas psychiatrists have traditionally condemned mysticists as purveyors of superstition, they share the basic belief that the mad person, unlike the sane person, does not choose or control his behaviors. They are controlled outside of himself, by godly powers, or from within, by involuntary biological forces. It is a fallacious premise in both forms and it has led followers of the medical model to distortions of reality as flagrant as those of mysticists.

BLEULER, CERLETTI, AND VONNEGUT

Consider the following typical descriptions of schizophrenia, quoted from Bleuler in a contemporary text:

> A remarkable number of events register on the minds of schizo-phrenics who are quite out of touch with reality. Many years after an event, a patient can produce minute details of what had occurred despite having been entirely self absorbed at the time . . . a schizophrenic who has appeared quite demented may, for example, suddenly produce a well integrated plan to escape from the hospital . . . a patient who at one moment can-not add 17 and 14 and at another can solve a difficult arithmetic problem is far more likely to be schizophrenic than mentally defective or suffering from brain damage.[3]

Let us be logical. If an individual can "produce minute details" of an event, he was not "out of touch with reality" at the time. He simply chose to appear that way. Similarly, one who concocts a "well integrated plan to escape from the hospital" is not "demented." And a person who can solve difficult arithmetic prob-lems, can tell the sum of 17 and 14 *whenever he so desires*.

Consider as well, again from archives retrieved by Szasz, the first report on the use of electroshock therapy in 1938, by Ugo Cerletti. Cerletti states that he began "cautiously," with brief, low voltage, whereupon the patient remained conscious and launched into loud song as soon as he recovered from the jolt. Then Cerletti and his colleagues decided to resume the following day using higher voltage. He reports:

All at once the patient, who had evidently been following our conversation, said clearly and solemnly without his usual gibberish: "Not another one! It's deadly!"[4]

The experiment continued nevertheless, and, not surprisingly, this first electroshock patient was "cured," as were millions to follow; that is, he refrained from that point from inappropriate singing or any behavior to attract the attention of his tormentors. It is truly incredible that from Cerletti's report to this day, the simplistic truth has not prevailed that if madness can be dispelled by the *anticipation* of shock therapy, then the premise underlying the therapy of a nonvolitional disease process must be entirely misconceived.

Finally, consider Mark Vonnegut. Vonnegut did not write as a mental-health professional, but as a former mental patient. His tale of his brief excursions with madness catapulted him from obscurity to the status of best-selling author alongside his famous father and the position of noted spokesperson for the medical model. He was not, however, flattering to psychiatrists in his book. For example:

> . . . doctors are always the last to catch on. The first to realize you've gotten better and start to treat you accordingly are the other patients. The realization flows up the hierarchy rather than down. After the patients catch on, then the maintenance staff and the lower orderlies realize you're O.K., and so on through the various orders of nurses until the news reaches the doctors.[5]

Nevertheless, the experience was sufficient for his conversion. In a postscript he tells us that he used to be "a Laing-Szasz fan and didn't believe there was really any such thing as schizophrenia," but he now realizes that it is "a very real disease." His experiences of "schizophrenia" are amusingly related. Some typical passages:

> One thing a tape of my ride to the hospital would show was how I was responding to outside events. It was a dialogue. I'd give some sort of blues rap and then there'd be some horn or something which was a "yes" or "amen" from all blues freaks. . . . Flashing neon signs and I had some very good raps. Jackhammers had some very encouraging things to say[6]

NOW IS THE TIME FOR GODS TO STAND UP FOR BAS-TARDS. The voices didn't even have the courtesy to tell me it was Shakespeare. As usual it seemed like the voices were trying to help, trying to give me some clues about what was going on. As usual, it didn't help much. Who was and who wasn't a bastard? What sort of things are gods and bastards going to do? When is now? [7]

One is led to accept the sincerity and fidelity of Vonnegut's descriptions. The conundrum, however, is: How can a mind that is disordered by disease keep an orderly account of it's own disorder? When he was "out-of-touch-with-reality," what part of him chronicled, in literate and engaging fashion, his interactions with reality? Sufferers of "real diseases" of the brain cannot render stimulating accounts of their own mental deterioration.

This is not to imply that Vonnegut, or the patients of Bleuler or Cerletti, did not feel as if they were out of control. But feeling out of control and being out of control are quite different. Lovers may feel out of control during an intense sexual encounter, but if a fire erupts alongside the bed they are not usually compelled to complete their activity. A heavy smoker may feel that he cannot control his habit, but if his physician tells him he is on the brink of lung disease, he will probably find that indeed he can. It is, in fact, an axiom of the human condition that we very often choose to believe that we cannot control our behavior. "I cannot help it," ranks among the most frequently uttered phrases in any language. "I cannot help" drinking, fornicating, brooding, fighting, mistrusting, withdrawing, rebelling, grieving, hurting the one I love, and on and on. It is figurative speech. It means, "I may have motives to change, but I have stronger motives to stay the same." When something convinces us to change our motives, we can and do change our feelings and beliefs and behavior, no matter how powerless to do so we may have previously felt. Most of us, deep in our hearts, are aware of this. Only psychiatrists take the metaphor seriously.

There is a general tendency to assign nonvolition to conditions and behaviors that cause conflict or pain, and volition to more pleasant states. We say, "My anxiety has returned," or, "I'm in a depression," or "I have an alcohol habit." We don't say, "My relaxation has returned," or, "I'm in a happiness," or, "I have a gourmet food habit." But our fears, moods, beliefs, and behaviors are controlled and controllable by our own intentions. They can only change if and when we decide to change them. This is not to imply that either the process of decision or change is necessarily easy. An intermediary may help by clarifying, suggesting, supporting, encouraging, and often coercing, but there is no intervention that can circumvent the person's own will. It is not a matter for "treatment." It is a matter for guidance, counselling, and teaching.

THE QUESTION OF PURPOSE

Not only does the medical model founder by virtue of its misconception, it effectively obstructs any feasible path to understanding madness. The psychiatrist sees someone huddled and weeping, or ranting and raving, or frightened to leave his bed, or speaking in an undecipherable manner, and he sees schizophrenia. He need not see or ask anymore, nor does he have anything to look for or ask about. It is a mysterious disease of undetermined origin.

If one truly strives to understand, he will see despair, or rage, or fear, or obfuscation. Thus, he has answerable questions to pose: What is the person sad about or fearful of? What prompts his excitement? Why doesn't he want to be understood? What does the behavior accomplish for him? What does it enable him to avoid?

The medical approach, in any form, does not allow such questions. The traditional medical concept of illness is that it is unequivocally maladaptive. It has no higher purpose, no larger reason for being than its own happening. Behavior, on the other hand, is always adaptive in some manner for the individual, always intelligible from the standpoint of a higher purpose, no matter how unreasonable it may appear. The wanton murderer acts to indulge his anger toward the world or to dispel his own sense of powerlessness, but killing is more satisfying for him than not killing, otherwise he would not kill. The voices inside people's heads are never random. They are always comprehensible in terms of some unresolved anxiety or conflict. They always symbolize something the person needs to deal with, which, for the sake of his own larger mental preservation, he does not acknowledge and contemplate by the customary modes of internal discourse that we call rational thought. "Loose associations" are generally loose only to the uninterested beholder. They usually harbor a message in metaphor, and the person always has a reason for choosing to communicate obliquely.

True, it is always easier to ascribe behavior to illness than to confront the relevant questions. After futile hours trying to elicit trust and cooperation from a delinquent child, it is probably tempting to call him a "sociopathic personality" and terminate the effort. Facing someone who claims to be God, it is far simpler to scribble "paranoid schizophrenia" in his file than to try to learn why he needs to tell you this.

Again, we see the parallel of the medical model and its mystical precursor. Both insulate us from any truths about madness, and thus, quite possibly, serve so-called rational man's interest in avoiding the recognition of his own potential to stray from sanity. We no longer isolate ourselves from madness by setting the insane adrift on "ships of fools," or by interning them in dungeons to be purged of devils, but we do confine them in what we euphemistically call "hospitals" to await fanciful cures for mythological diseases.

MAKING THE MAD PERSON MADDER

The misplaced premises of the medical model not only deter us from discovering truths, they underlie the practices of the professions that serve to keep the mad person mad, and they often make him madder. These practices stem from the concept that the mental patient is not responsible for what he does. The concept is based on another inappropriate analogy to somatic medicine: that the mental patient is no more accountable for or obliged to modify his behavior than the medical patient is accountable for or obliged to modify his tumor or virus. Just as is the victim of any other disease, the mental patient is incapable of knowing or getting what he needs. He must, to be cured of his mental illness, relinquish his decision-making powers, in matters small and large, to the doctor and the institution.

Generally, the somatic sufferer willingly and tolerably accepts this invalidation of himself as an expert on his own bodily functions. For the mental patient, however, it is an invalidation of himself as a person. His words, thoughts, desires, intentions, beliefs, attitudes, actions, are all deemed of dubious value. As an exercise in the psychological infantilization of adult human beings, the mental hospital has no parallel in modern society. Whatever the bases were for the feelings of helplessness or inadequacy that led the mental patient to his madness, his treatment represents the supreme substantiation of them.

Fortunately, from what I have seen, a large number of mental patients, mad or otherwise, are more aware about themselves than their professionals. In mental hospitals, patients form a subculture with attitudes and beliefs about their problems that are quite divergent from and more valid than those of the professional staff subculture.[8] Many others, however, are more vulnerable and do accept this ultimate declaration of their own unworthiness. That is often sufficient to assure their continued careers as mad people, and the establishment is thus afforded another method of creating its own self-fulfilling prophecies about the durability of mental illness and the ongoing deterioration of the afflicted.

MOTIVES FOR MADNESS:
An Inquiry into Oblique Intentions

SICK? NO! CRAZY? YES!

Although it retards meaningful communication to think of people as mentally ill, there are perfectly good terms such as *mad, crazy, insane, off the wall, bonkers,* and so on, that usually show consensus. Neither professionals nor the public can concur with one another about the presence of neurosis, psychosis, schizophrenia, or the like, but people do seem to agree about whether someone is acting crazy or not.

With my students, I have tried to render their implicit definitions explicit, without much success. If we relinquish the fallacious concepts of nonvolition and nonpurposiveness, attempts to define madness become highly subjective. The closest I have come to a generalization is: behavior for which the observer cannot conceive an intelligible motive. Thus, shooting strangers is sane if it is part of one's tasks as soldier or revolutionary, insane as independent activity. Ritualistic behavior is O.K. within religious or fraternal ceremonies, but not outside of these. Severe anxiety or depression become madness only if there is no observable cause.

The absence of formal definition did not deter Otto Freidrich from his superb accounts of the histories of people who had "gone crazy." In fact, after succinctly dismissing psychiatric definitions, he concluded that, nevertheless, "we know perfectly well what we are talking about."[1] If the social science–minded reader cannot abide an inquiry into something without an operational definition, however, the present exercise may be viewed as simply trying to find motives where there are none apparent.

LIFE-EXPERIENCE THEORIES

Though Freidrich's journalistic eye was keen, he did not emerge with new answers. He uncovered as many unique histories as he had cases, and his conclusions were some vague comments about "unhappy childhoods" leading to "unhappy marriages" and "unhappy jobs."

Unhappy childhoods is the theme, as well, in the theories of those few professionals who disassociated themselves from the medical model sufficiently enough to pursue valid inquiries about madness. Notable among these are Gregory Bateson, Jay Haley, and Ronald Laing.[2] All used the term "schizophrenia" – with avowed reluctance and with disclaimers about its status as a medical concept – to refer, mainly, to irrational beliefs and deviant modes of communication. All maintained, essentially, that there is a particular pattern of parenting that produces madness of this nature: unloving, confusing, scapegoating, rife with ambiguous and contradictory responses and demands, bereft of conditions for the development of trust in self or others. Madness serves as a shield, a protection against the overwhelming feeling of anxiety that results from the absence of self-identity and esteem.

One does encounter cases that seem to leap from the pages of Bateson and Haley and Laing. The problem is that one also frequently finds distorted beliefs and communications in young people and in individuals many decades removed from their childhoods without any evidence of such parenting patterns.

Another life-experience theory, by Martin Seligman, provides a plausible analysis of severe, prolonged depression as an expression of "learned helplessness"[3]; that is, a series of failures to effect desired outcomes that eventuate in pervasive pessimism and dependency. But, again, some depressed persons are prototypes of this model, whereas others appear to have been highly successful in achieving goals large and small, and most do not fit without ambiguity on either pole.

The contributions of these writers and some others in revealing some of the adaptive functions of madness represent the sole light in nearly 100 years of darkness. The specifics of their individual theories, however, are far less encompassing than they may appear.

The professional who toils in the world of the mad will inevitably find that there is no one set of principles that applies universally, unless he is highly selective in his cases or brings his own biases to bear upon them. There are generalities that seem to pertain here and there. They may come from one of the aforementioned researchers or from a diversity of behavioral-science sources, ranging from the psychoanalytic theories of Freud and Erikson to the conditioning model of B. F. Skinner. In the real world, however, every case is virtually a theory unto itself. The professional must be more detective than practitioner, relying on curiosity and intuition, and ready to take necessary risks to pursue his hypotheses when they require blatant meddling in the lives of his charges.

The detective analogy is also congruent to the search for motives, which is basic to every case. Why is the person being crazy? What does the craziness accomplish? Sometimes the question will lead directly to the life history, sometimes it will not. The professional may find some common threads among the motives he uncovers for different cases, but they will be no more than that: some common threads. Each pattern will tend to be more unique than similar to the others.

MADNESS AS ROLE

There is one thread that had become apparent to me in many of the cases I have seen. In those cases, the madness appears to be a role, a mode of self-presentation that has become part of the person's self-identity. Just like any other role, it is adopted because it meets the person's needs, in terms of both his ongoing interpersonal relationships and his definition of self-in-relation-to-others.

The film *Taxi Driver* provides an insightful dramatization of the process. The warrior returned from Vietnam finds that he is no longer a hero, and he cannot find a satisfactory alternative role. He attracts women of all stripe, but, confused about the nuances of courtship, he clumsily attempts to seduce a career woman and to reform a prostitute, but is unceremoniously re-jected by both. Nor can he reconcile his vocation as taxi driver to his self-concept. Gradually he forms the conviction that the evils of the world are at the core of his frustrations, and he adopts the role of vigilante, spending hours at a time rehearsing heroic scenarios. Eventually, he passes the point where fantasy is sufficient, and he sets out to assassinate a young, successful politician whom the career woman admires. But, thwarted prior to the assassination attempt, he turns, instead, upon a glib, facile pimp who holds the slavish affections of the prostitute, and kills him and several of his gangster associates. In the ironic finale, the taxi driver emerges a public hero. He returns to his taxi and to the adulation of friends and strangers with new-found poise, confidence, and self-satisfaction, his madness apparently dispelled for as long as his new role meets his needs.

The paramount indication that madness serves as role is when its expression seems primarily directed to others, usually significant others, most often family. It is manifested in a manner by which others are unavoidably engulfed by it. Some illustrations from cases I have dealt with follow:

- Belinda, a woman in her late twenties, was escorted to my office by an entourage of kin who, in turn, described to me how she had recently begun to bury household objects in her yard, boil articles of her husband's clothing, set small sterno fires throughout their home, and proclaim, to anyone who would listen, that her husband had hired someone to try to seduce her so he could obtain a divorce. The husband had just read a book and suggested that she was either compulsive neurotic or schizophrenic. A sister believed her behavior was somehow related to their late father's cruelty. Her mother was convinced that her daughter was possessed by the devil. Belinda listened to all of this complacently and commented only that a voice in her head, which she thought might be God, instructed her to do these things.
- Mark was preceded into my office by his parents, who characterized him as having much potential, but impeded by a long-standing "schizophrenic" condition. In the five years since high school graduation, he had not sustained himself in a job or educational program. At first, he would profess disaffection with whatever he was doing and would return to the family home to watch television most of the night and sleep most of the day. His parents refused to have him home on one occasion, and retrieved him shortly thereafter from a mental hospital, where he had arrived after informing coworkers of a constant noise in

his head. From that point, his sojourns from home became shorter and less frequent and his behavior took on an added element: his complaints about the noise ceased, but he varied his television and sleep schedule by drawing elaborate blueprints for a family bomb shelter, in anticipation of imminent nuclear war, that he hung from the walls of the home. His parents came to see me when they discovered that he had purchased materials for its construction with his father's credit card.

- The Batemans were a retired couple in their sixties. Mrs. Bateman had been in two mental hospitals for short stays during the prior two years, based on her delusion, with which she regularly harangued Mr. Bateman, that he was sneaking out of the house nightly after she was asleep, in order to conduct an affair with a neighbor. Their children, whom I interviewed, found the alleged liaison difficult to conceive and, because their mother was a light sleeper, thought it improbable that their father could leave and return undetected. Mr. Bateman insisted that his wife was well aware that he had been rendered impotent by prostatic surgery during the entire time in question.

- Evelyn, in her early fifties, was brought to me by her husband Martin, during a recurrence of her "chronic, severe depression." According to Martin, she wept and moaned constantly, called him several times a day at his office, made many references to suicide, and paced the house nightly with all of the lights on until he awakened and sat up with her.

When madness is role, as in these cases, the person usually appears more bothersome than bothered. Thus, Belinda was most benign about her hallucinations: God or whomever had something to say to her and that was that. Both Mark and Mrs. Bateman perceived that their problems resided in their families' refusals to recognize or acknowledge the truth. Evelyn felt that her major source of difficulty was Martin's unwillingness to tolerate her "illness."

At the outset, then, the professional should not expect much meaningful cooperation from the client. Others often become important sources of information.

After a largely uncommunicative session with Belinda, I decided to interview each of her family members privately. It was a sibling who informed me of Belinda's husband's "insane jealousy" and his total domination of her to the point of monitoring every hour of her schedule when he was at work, forbidding her to leave his side in public without permission, and the like. My informant believed that the man in Belinda's seduction fantasy corresponded, in some way, to a man her husband had actually hired to spy on her while he was away. I eventually learned from Belinda that her madness began a short while after she had made an atypical outburst of protest to her husband, which was met by a beating and a threat that he would leave her homeless and penniless, and that he would tell everyone she knew of her alleged wayward behavior.

The rationale for Mark's madness began to unfold in a series of private sessions with him and with each of his parents. In his father's eyes, Mark had an unrealized "potential" to become the engineer that Mark's father had always aspired to be. The father's ambition for his son had been the focal point of their relationship since Mark was a child. The flaw in the plan, however, was that Mark had little aptitude or inclination for the physical sciences. Thus, after struggling to achieve average high school grades, he plodded through several failing semesters in various universities, interspersed with construction and apprentice draftsman jobs, which, his father constantly reminded him, merely represented pauses in his career until he could "get himself together."

I learned from Mr. Bateman's physician that his impotence was probably more psychological than physical in origin. His surgery did, however, herald a period of marked diminution of sexual activity, which eventually became none at all, accompanied, Mr. Bateman admitted, by a withdrawal of affectional attention of any kind on his part toward his wife. I gradually elicited Mrs. Bateman's feelings of hurt and anger, about both her husband's distance and her perceptions of previous signs of indifference and rejection throughout their marriage.

The thirty-odd year marriage of Evelyn and Martin had always been stereotypically traditional. She assumed all of the household chores and responsibilities; he earned all of the money and made all of the major decisions unilaterally. Evelyn maintained that she felt this was the way it should be, and complained little when a decision was not to her liking, but it was during these times that she exhibited her depressed behaviors. The episode presented above began shortly after Martin sold their home, where she was secure and comfortable, and they had moved to another city for reasons concerning his career. Evelyn's depressions invariably eventuated in private hospitalization, whereby Martin became very upset, about both the costs and the necessity for him to care for himself and the family.

In each of these cases, the mad role provided the person, albeit in a rather perverse way, the means to relieve some specific source of frustration. Belinda found a way to assert her will, though it had to be in the form of God's will speaking through her. Mark could remain dependent at home and avoid the tyranny of his father's ambitions and the admission of his own failings: he was, after all, mad. Mrs. Bateman kept her husband's attention, kept it, in fact, rooted upon her. Evelyn made Martin the silent, suffering slave to her needs, at least for a time.

In this vein, the three delusions become meaningful as ironic distortions of the perceived oppressions. The oppression was acknowledged, but in a manner in which direct confrontation was avoided and the oppressor was frustrated, in turn, by virtue of his own behavior. The man Belinda's husband had appointed guardian of her virtue became a seducer hired by him; his most feared prophecy thereby fulfilled by his own hand. Mark became an engineer of sorts after all, his blueprints displayed for all the family to admire. Mrs. Bateman had always been mightily wounded and chagrinned by Mr. Bateman's flirtatious attentions toward other women, but too fearful of the possibility that he might leave her to react directly. Now he was being made to pay for his game without the opportunity to play. Evelyn didn't need a delusion. She achieved poetic justice everytime she embarked for the hospital and evoked Martin's displeasure.

It is not unusual to find such meaning and function in delusions, which is, perhaps, why they frequently show common themes. When people tell me about being controlled by fanciful, alien forces, I look for the controlling forces in their lives. When they claim to be Jesus Christ, I seek to learn who it is they feel is martyring them.

CHANGING ROLE CONSEQUENCES

Psychiatrist John Rosen achieved prominence in the late 1950s with a method for dealing with the maddest of the mad called "direct analysis." [4] It was a euphemism for "unmitigated intimidation," but with Rosen's imposing frame and manner and the coterie of "co-therapists" who accompanied him, it generally worked. To a lad who claimed that he recalled hearing a radio broadcast of jazz music on the way home from the hospital when he was born, Rosen replied, ". . . you think you could know that when you were a week old. You make me sick with your lies . . . I never heard such craziness." To a woman with the secret information that Russian soldiers had infiltrated the United States: "Would you rather talk about Russia or your real problem? What's your real problem? . . . [to the co-therapists] Funny how all the Russia cases try to make believe it's something else." As did most of Rosen's reported cases, both reverted to sanity almost immediately. Rosen and the lad then talked about why he needed to fantasize a life-long association with jazz. The woman began to describe the "other woman" who had infiltrated her marriage. It was reputed in the mental health grapevine of two decades ago that Rosen occasionally screamed in the ear of mute patients until they spoke to him, and had various similar methods of gaining attention.

Rosen's successes are perfectly explicable within the concept of madness-as-role. As deeply ingrained as any role may be, people appear very capable of shifting abruptly out of it when it fails to elicit desired effects. The iconoclast who engenders scorn might readily adopt a more normative public posture. The party-clown usually quiets down rapidly if he is ignored.

I made an interesting discovery some years ago. I watched John, a mental patient who had been home briefly from the hospital, befuddle his family, the police, and a crisis worker with blatherings about the CIA and such. When, during one of my seminars-in-a-madhouse, I encountered him about a month later among his fellow patients, he appeared to be perfectly sane. Finally, I asked him about his behavior at our prior encounter. John looked embarrassed, and one of the others said, with a smile, "He tried that one time, but we don't listen to that stuff here." As a rule, schizophrenics do not talk schizophrenic to other schizophrenics. The role doesn't make much of an impact.

Most of us do not possess the temperament, demeanor, or staff of dutiful co-therapists to replicate Rosen's techniques precisely, but direct confrontation can be used constructively in a variety of ways. Based on the concept that mad people are not aware of or in control of their behavior, professionals tend to approach them very passively. Professionals become, in a sense, accomplices to the role, nodding their acceptance of distorted beliefs, letting obscure responses go by without comment. But the mad person knows he is being mad, and knows that the professional knows. The only way to coax him out of the role is not to get into it with him.

Thus, with people who speak to me in metaphor or in "loose association," I generally reply that I know that what they say has meaning, but I cannot understand their meaning, and I cannot help them unless I do understand them. If they want to hold my attention—that is, if they perceive that I am an advocate and not a threat—they usually "clear," in the clinical parlance, with amazing alacrity. It is, of course, beneficial for me to have the means available to demonstrate both advocacy and a capacity to help.

To a man I encountered at a police station, who had had a violent outburst at home and had insisted, as I knew he had on similar occasions, that he was someone else, I said, "Joseph, I know you are in there somewhere, and I need you to talk to me if I am going to get you out of jail and into a hospital." He looked at me warily for a moment, then began to question me about what hospital and for how long.

When I was associated with a group home for children, I was charged with assessing the suitability for admission of a teen-aged lad, who was otherwise slated to return to the mental hospital where he had previously spent several months. He responded to most of my questions by whispered consultations into a pocket radio that he claimed linked him to his colleagues on another planet. After a few minutes of this, I put my face, eyeball to eyeball, about six inches from his (a splendid way to get someone's attention) and asked, "Roger, do you want to go back to the hospital?" He shook his head.

"Well, then, you have got to talk straight to me, because I have to decide whether you go back there, or to another place that you'll like much better and have more freedom." Silence. But he kept his radio at his side.

"Roger, I don't know if you really believe you are talking to another planet, and I don't care right now, but when you do that, it frightens people. I think you know that. Now, I will see that you go into a home and not the hospital, if you can promise me that you will not do that or anything else that will frighten people for two weeks. Can you promise that?"

"I think so," he said; then, after a pause, "I started doing this to show off or something. . . . Now, I'm not sure whether it's real or not."

Roger, incidentally, kept his promise to the letter: exactly two weeks later he was back in contact with the planet. Eventually, however, we were able to help him find more enduring motives for sanity and he turned out quite well.

GIVING UP THE ROLE

Needless to say, when the professional has established the motives for madness and made meaningful contact with his client, his tasks have merely begun. Then he must inspire and aid the person to adopt saner roles: to confront frustrations in more direct manner. At its simplest, it is a far more arduous task than labelling and drugging. Successes do not generally come easy, nor can they be achieved in any fixed manner.

Of the four cases described previously, Belinda responded most readily. At my urging, she left home shortly to live with a sister and promptly relinquished her rituals. My role, then, was to help her build on the self-esteem and autonomy that she did already possess, that had enabled her to lodge her protest in madness. (Many after all, never become sane enough to confront oppression, even in an insane manner.) A vocational counselor whom I brought into the case was a key factor, by putting her on a path toward economic independence for the first time in her life. Within six months, and after one abortive attempt at reconciliation with her husband, she was living successfully on her own.

Mark was a more difficult matter. His sense of personal failure extended beyond career considerations to most aspects of his perceived manhood. His dependency on his parents was coupled with a rage toward them so intense that it could only be expressed in the most oblique terms of his warnings of nuclear holocaust. Mark led me to these insights slowly and grudgingly, for though we struck a bargain early to exclude the topics of nuclear war and bomb shelters from our conversations, this left little else that he wanted to discuss. Finally, I convinced his parents to coerce him to accept my offer of an institutional, group living arrangement, with emphasis on social rehabilitation. There, after an initial period of hostility toward me for forcing his exodus from the home, he became somewhat more responsive. I was able to elicit some expressions of his anger toward his parents, and there was some movement on his part toward perceiving his failures as part of a self-learning process rather than as inevitable consequences of intrinsic, personal inadequacy. But the risk of relinquishing his mad role only to find failure anew was still very frightening to him. One love affair is worth a thousand counselling hours, and a young, assertive woman, who arrived at the center and found in Mark some answers to her own problems, took him the rest of the way. He returned to see me, with his bride, about a year later. He had many problems, still, but was coping at a far more constructive level than nuclear war fantasies.

With the Batemans, I tried to bring each to an understanding of their own and the other's anxieties and frustrations, and to effect some arrangement for them to cohabit in mutual tolerance, at the least. Mr. Bateman seemed ready. Mrs. Bateman, unwilling to foresake the power and vengeance bestowed by her mad role, clearly was not. One time only did she allow me past her delusion. During a particularly volatile joint session, after she accused Mr. Bateman of long-standing, unrequited lust for the neighbor in question, I suggested, gently, "Then you know that he isn't really sneaking out to see her." She replied, "Well, he would if he could." Finally I informed them that I could not help them further and that, perhaps, there was simply too much water under the bridge for them to live peaceably with one another again. Mr. Bateman rose and thanked me, as if this was what he had been waiting to hear, and strode out. Mrs. Bateman sat quietly for a few seconds; then, with a sudden look of fear, she left without a word to follow him. I heard from Mr. Bateman several months later. He had, in fact, left her for a time, but returned in response to her contrite pleas. Their conflicts were less frequent and intense and, though the matter of the neighbor arose on occasion, it had retreated from the forefront of their relationship. Mr. Bateman wanted to know if there was any way Mrs. Bateman could now be conclusively "cured" of her delusion. I informed him that I thought this was the best things were going to be for a while.

I accomplished virtually nothing for Evelyn and Martin. I believed she wanted nothing from me but agent services for her planned hospital excursion. When she realized it was not going to come easily or without conditions, she found it elsewhere and I did not hear from them again.

PUBLIC AND PRIVATE MADNESS

Madness is not always a role; in fact, there are cases which seem almost counterpoints to those above. Some individuals appear to take pains *not* to include others in their madness or even to reveal its innermost nature. Three illustrations follow:

- Robert was referred to me following his discharge from a psychiatric ward, with a notation in his file cautioning me about his reticence to discuss his problems. Haltingly and painfully, he described to me the admonishing "voices inside his head" and the compulsive rituals they demanded of him; for example, crossing himself a specified number of times, saying sections of the Scriptures aloud. He was in his late thirties, and he had lived most of his life alone. He performed his rituals as discreetly as he could, and the only people he had ever taken into his confidence – during several visits to mental hospitals to seek help – were professionals and a few fellow patients.
- Deborah arrived at my office after cancelling two prior appointments, and immediately elicited my assurance that none of her family would learn that she had been there. With the aid of tranquilizers, which she took covertly, she had managed to keep her husband and teen-aged children from realizing the frequency and intensity of her depressed and anxious states. Deborah had confided in a friend, who urged her to find counselling, but she was skeptical that anyone could help her if she could not, herself.
- James also came without the knowledge of his family, and was most eager to convey to me that he had always been perfectly normal until his recent problem. Then he described, with obvious discomfort, the terrifying fears he experienced whenever he was alone with his first-born, three-year-old son that he would accidentally, or deliberately, through loss of self-control, hurt the child. James assured me that he loved his wife and son, and appeared extremely distraught about the effect this had on his relationship with both, for he was loath to confide in his wife, but made efforts to avoid the child unless she was nearby.

The expressions of madness are often similar when madness is role and when it is not. Voices, compulsive rituals, and depression were shared by both public and private types in these illustrations. In the main, however, delusions and obscure communication tend to be the province of madness-as-role; specific and generalized anxieties and obsessive thinking are more common where it is private. Whatever the expressions, however, the experience of madness-as-role appears to be quite different from that of private madness. When it is role, the madness has been assimilated into the self-concept; when it is private, it has not: not only is it regarded as unacceptable in the person's interactions with others, it is perceived as something alien to his very nature. Private types are thus far more uncomfortable with themselves and far more committed to change. As a rule of thumb, in fact, the more resistant a client appears to change, the more likely it is that the madness has become incorporated into role.

The guiding question, however, remains the same: What does the madness accomplish for the person? For the public type, the answer involves a conflict with others. For the private type, the conflict is within the individual, and is, generally, more deeply rooted in the person's life history.

Robert was raised by elderly grandparents who were deeply fundamentalist in their religious beliefs, oblivious to the developmental needs, passions, and curiosities of a growing child. Virtually everything Robert did and every thought he expressed, apart from dutiful attention to his Bible, schoolwork, and chores, provoked warnings of hell-fires and brimstone and ceremonial punishments, many of them similar to his later compulsive acts. Robert's grandparents dominated his socialization. He was the only other person on their farm, school equally constrained his expression, and he had neither access to, nor time for, peers. When his grandparents both died in rapid succession in his fourteenth year, Robert went to live with other relatives, where adults were rarely home and the children knew few boundaries to their behavior. His new options fascinated but terrified him. The older children coerced him into some homosexual and heterosexual experimentation, which evoked in him such an overwhelming sense of evil and anxiety that he needed to literally revive his grandparents' voices and rituals of redemption. He never retreated from this mode of adjustment.

Deborah was abandoned by both parents, one following the other, as a young child, and lived in a series of relatives' and foster homes. She married at seventeen with one purpose in mind: security. Her husband had never provided much in the way of companionship or physical satisfaction and was not particularly sensitive or attentive to her. But she had always been certain he would not leave her: he simply was not the type. She devoted herself to motherhood for eighteen years, and when her children no longer depended on her, she began to despair. She thought of ending the marriage, but the notion of risking her security was still frightening. Thus, she took herself through cycles of depression and anxiety, each creating the conditions for the other. She expressed to me her frequent wish that her husband would somehow leave her, much as a person embarking on a first parachute jump might desire a push to force resolution of a painful conflict.

James had not been abandoned as a child, though he probably would have been advantaged if he had. His drunkard father regularly abused both him and his mother physically. His mother used James for sympathy and succor when she needed to, but would often, unpredictably, align with her husband against him. Thus, James never developed trust in the validity of his own feelings about either of his parents' responses to him and consequently never expressed, outwardly or to himself, his hatred of them. Nor did he recognize the self-hatred he felt for his own powerlessness. He coped with this in adolescence by devoting himself slavishly to muscle-building and the martial arts, and maintained his adjustment sufficiently to leave home for the military as soon as he was of age and to find a compatible mate and a job upon his return. The child is father to the man, however, and as his son grew to an age where James began to project his own child-self onto him, and where James began to identify, as well, in his paternal role with his own father, his long-repressed ambivalances came to the fore. Part of him despised his son's vulnerability and dependency, as he had despised his own. At the same time, he could not directly accept any feelings of frustration or anger toward the child, for they evoked images of his own father within himself.

Dealing with private madness, I find that I follow a similar credo of confrontation as with public madness; that is, when I form an explanation for the function of the behavior, I strive, without creating undue stress, to share it with the client. Simplistic as this may seem, it is nevertheless antithetical to most approaches. Even those that are not based on biological concepts tend to view aberrance as involuntary: somehow remote from the person's "rational" will and intention. The professional, perhaps following the role model of the physician, maintains a lofty distance from the client, keeping his insights to himself and using his expertise to try to manipulate whatever hypothetical process his theory deems at the source: "object relations," "character armor," or "security dynamism," for example. A cynical essay by Jay Haley views the interaction of client and professional within this approach as an ongoing contest of "one upmanship."[5]

Often, the revelation of a source serves in itself to ease the problem. A commonly reported expression of madness in the early Freudian era, *hysterical conversion reaction* (dysfunction or paralysis of some bodily system without apparent organic cause) is virtually extinct today, and the most plausible explanation is that an increasing sophistication of the populace about the nature and dynamics of subconscious motivation has rendered it ineffective in its function as a symbolic expression of conflict. The question is: What are all those folks doing who would have developed hysterical conversion reactions at the turn of the century?

The interpretation of the medical model that contemporary Freudians adopt in their concept of "symptom substitution" is that an illness cannot be cured by abetting its symptoms, for the illness will manifest itself in some other way. Within the present framework, however, there is no intrinsic predisposition of mad people toward perverse behaviors or feeling states. The perversity occurs because they find it difficult to accept and deal directly with some major conflict. Lead, coerce, induce, compel them to, and the function and form of the madness will dissipate.

Thus, once Deborah began to verbalize to herself what it was that she was in despair of and frightened about, her diffuse, emotional reactions became focussed on the facts of her conflict, and she began to deal with them more concretely. I tried to help her in this by supportive counselling and by encouraging some role-playing directed at the origins of her anxiety. I encouraged her, for example, to privately act out scenarios in which she confronted her husband about her unhappiness, or fantasized about being separated from him. She didn't actually leave her marriage during the period of our sessions – she did about a year later – but she was more content and secure when we concluded.

James was more reticent in response to my probings and interpretations of his background. I could not, in fact, fathom the affect of our talks until one session, wherein he described to me with great satisfaction how he had confronted his parents during the previous week, unburdening himself of a quarter-century of resentments and concluding with the proclamation that he felt fortunate that he was he and not either of them. He continued this catharsis in our further sessions, and, for my part, I tried to assure that he often reminded himself that he was, indeed, he and not either of them. He eventually shared his problems and insights with his wife and gained her tolerance and support. Gradually he relinquished his obsessions, settled into normal parenthood and could even, to an extent, forgive his parents and accept them for what they were.

With Robert, I tried first to change his concept about "the voices." Rather than an affliction or a disease, as they had been described to him by other professionals, I wanted him to view the voices as his own willful expressions, based on some deep-seated conflicts. As with the others, I explored with him the origins of his conflicts, and encouraged him to reenact the traumas of his childhood with a more benevolent perception of his own childhood needs and feelings. In dealing with the present, I urged him to answer the alien-seeming voices from the part of him that strived for autonomy and I urged him to give acceptance and expression, in his fantasies if not yet in behavior, to the impulses and desires that evoked the censor in him. I found him the most deeply troubled and acutely pained of the three described here. I had about a month with him, then he left to take residence with relatives in another state. Perhaps we could have accomplished more with more time – perhaps not – but I heard that he eventually returned to the mental-institutional system for what appeared to be a prolonged basis.

DEMEANOR DISORDER

There are other types I have encountered who would have to be characterized as mixed in regard to the public-private dimension. I have noticed one of these types around universities more than anywhere else; perhaps because it is a tolerant setting. They function well, often at a reasonably high level, and appear earnestly to want to be liked and accepted. The problem is that they are consistently inappropriate. As in madness-as-role, the individual doesn't believe he is crazy, but others do. The madness, however, is not primarily oriented to some specific interpersonal need; thus, the person is not indifferent to, nor righteous about, his effects on others. He is usually aware that something is wrong, and would dearly like to change it, but doesn't have a clue as to how to begin.

Some are notable for their non sequiturs, particularly in casual exchanges. Once, I stopped the department eccentric after he had responded to my passing nod with some smiling gibberish, and asked him precisely what he meant. He was embarrassed, but seemed almost grateful, and he did explain. It was an extremely oblique reference to the weather, and I realized that his non sequiturs were simply misguided attempts at banter. We usually take them for granted, but the allegory, metaphor, and jest that characterize our daily small talk are very delicate skills. My friend lacked the knack, though he possessed a different sort of humor in a different context, but he perceived badinage as a necessary human endeavor and, inasmuch as his sense of the figurative was a little askew, he was not quite sure why his attempts did not generate the same reactions as other folk's.

Others of this type seem to miss completely the nuances of nonverbal signals. They interrupt when you are warming up to the point, and wait in rapt attention after you have finished. They stand too close or too far away or both, alternately. Their frowns are too intense; their smiles too broad; their eye contact either too brief or sustained. They are very difficult to deal with. If you are at all hospitable, they will, henceforth, hover at your elbow. If you show displeasure about this, they will abandon you completely except for a pained scowl when you pass.

Sociologist Erving Goffman referred to "psychotics and other cut-ups" who violate the rules of "decorum and demeanor that regulate face-to-face interaction." [6] I think that the behavior does sometimes take on this role component: the actor gains both license and attention, but primarily there is a true gap, for whatever cause, in the development of interpersonal skills. If you engender the person's trust, he will usually be quite receptive to

"demeanor" or "style retraining," which can be very broadly defined. With the lad I questioned in the hallway, who came to my
office several days later to talk about why no one seems to understand him, we simply decided, mutually, that banter wasn't his
thing. He ceased the effort, began to respond, with some coach-
ing, in straightforward manner in casual interactions (which
proved to have a certain charm of its own), and he gradually went
from "dip" to "serious, but nice fellow" in the public eye. The gross-
est non sequitur of all, it turned out, was by a clinical psychologist
on the faculty who described him to colleagues as a "schizophrenic
in spontaneous remission."

MASTERS AND MISTRESSES OF METAPHOR

A second mixed type is a counterpoint to the first, in that the
sense of symbol appears over- rather than under-developed. This
madness is manifest almost totally in the verbal domain. Those of
this type are masters and mistresses of metaphor, bounding about
in figurative heights with an alacrity that defies the most imagina-
tive mental-health professional to follow. If their talents were
channelled, they could be acknowledged poets and poetesses. Psychologist Ira Cohen presented a selection from Joyce in juxtaposition with so-called "psychotic" writing of this nature, to illustrate
that they were indistinguishable.[7]
    Again there is an aspect of role for this type. The individual
can turn these flights of allegory on or off at will, and often does so
to manipulate the environment. In this vein, it is often used as a
test of whether others are *really* interested or clever enough to
understand him. As Jay Haley depicted in another amusing piece,
clinicians usually fail ignominiously.[8] On the other hand, if you
earn their confidence and straight talk, they will describe frequent, intense states of fear and sadness.
    These seem to be the mad sorts that have primarily attracted
the attention of the aforementioned life-experience theorists. I
have found, however, that this is a quite rare type, and I sometimes suspect that most who exist manage to make their way into
some textbook. As I suggested, I have also grown skeptical of the
premise of homogeneous life experiences. If you try, you can pro-

ject almost anyone's theory into almost any household, but I doubt whether a properly controlled, empirical study would show that, as a group, in general, the parenting of people of this type was unique in any concrete, predictable regard.

What they do seem to have in common is a finely tuned "crap detector"; that is, they can perceive with remarkable astuteness beyond language to actual motives and meanings, which may be part of their general sensitivity to symbol. Otherwise, their verbal madness can be looked at in the same context as delusions, hallucinations, or compulsive rituals, as indirect but meaningful expressions of fears, angers, and frustrations. As with our earlier illustrations, in order to discover the specifics of the fears, angers, and frustrations, each case must be approached as a theory unto itself.

FUNCTION VS. FORM

I have offered perspectives rather than models and techniques. This, I believe, is the current state of the art. My focus has been on the intelligibility of madness: on its adaptive functions, and the role of the professional in discovering these and leading the client to less obtuse and more beneficial ways of dealing with himself and the world. In my illustrations of adaptive functions of madness and means of effecting change, I have borrowed from such diverse and, often, antithetical, sources as Freud, Laing, Haley, Rosen, Perls, Ellis, and the Behaviorists, with a healthy infusion of conventional wisdom.

The emphasis has been ideographic rather than nomothetic, on individuals rather than classifications. In place of the myriad medical categories, the varieties of neuroses, psychoses, and character disorders, I have provided madness-as-role and madness-alien-to-role, and several types for whom even this somewhat ambiguous dichotomy does not seem to pertain. In this vein I have attended more to the nature of the individual's conflict than to the particular way he chooses to express it; that is, to the function of madness rather than the form.

Both professionals and the public, in my estimation, have been unduly enchanted by forms of madness. The prevailing concept is that such modes of thought and behavior are qualitatively different from normal. The differences, however, are more feasibly viewed on a quantitative dimension and are not as esoteric as they are made to appear.

Let the reader try to peer into his own, ongoing thought processes. Generally, they are less akin to an editorial column than to the disjointed flow of associations ascribed to madness. In fact, the literary appeal of stream-of-consciousness writing is that it reveals this aspect of ourselves.

Is hallucinating more than an intense form of imagining? All of us conjure images and hold conversations in our minds daily.

In regard to delusions, there is some Walter Mitty in everyone, and probably more than a few have experienced times when the fantasy became so intense that the boundary of reality blurred momentarily, or they found themselves describing the myth as if it were fact. And who has not held unrealistic beliefs? My own favorite is that I will someday write a famous novel, undaunted by the harsh realities that I have not, in the near half-century of my life, published a line of fiction, nor made any kind of reasonable effort in pursuit of my desire.

Are there many whose thoughts have not run, in times of stress, toward obsession, or whose behavior has not taken on a compulsive character? Who is totally unfamiliar with the experience of depression, or manic excitement? Even the exotic *dissociative reaction* (amnesia) has a counterpart in the normal: it is called *perceptual defense* and it refers to the adaptive exclusion from conscious awareness of threatening stimuli, which appears to be part of our general pattern of response to the world.

Why then impart mystique to those for whom such facets of mind may have become more intense or prolonged, or who may have chosen to bring them from the periphery to the forefront of experience, or who may have simply decided to make them public. The facets, themselves, comprise the riddles of mind in all of its expressions. It is conceivable, though not apparent by any means, that when solutions are at hand, useful classifications of forms of madness will emerge. For the present and foreseeable future, however, the meaningful questions appear to be in terms of function.

THE PROFESSIONAL

These perspectives demand more than a revised conceptual orientation on the part of the professional. They require significant changes in self-identity and role. Many who eschew the overt trappings of the medical model, that is, the diagnostic categories, pseudobiological theories, and so forth, nevertheless engage in doctoring. They receive their patients in their offices, on fixed schedules, where they administer therapies, if not in the form of chemicals, then in the form of other definitive techniques – for example, free association; transactional analysis; unqualified, positive regard; transmutation of biopsychic energies. They treat and the patient is treated. They dispense and the patient is dispensed to. The flow is largely one-way, and that is, of course, the essence of doctoring.

The approach to madness as a volitional, adaptive process does not lend itself to doctoring. Professional and client need to be partners in a mutual exploration of the client's conflicts, motives, modes of adjustment. Sometimes the professional will lead and the client will follow; sometimes the client will lead and the professional will follow. Sometimes the professional will question the client's interpretation, and the question may be valid or not. Sometimes the client will question the professional's interpretation, and that question may be valid or not. If an analogy for the relationship is desired, the professional is more like a wilderness guide than a doctor to a client. His expertise may reside in knowing some truer paths and pitfalls, but they must both go up the mountain together. Like wilderness exploration, it is usually best if there are not fixed rules of procedure for the journey. It is often as exhausting an enterprise.

The doctoring model is inadequate in other regards, as well. To meddle effectively in the ongoing crises of others, the professional will frequently need to depart from his office and schedule, to observe or intervene first-hand. Particularly with children and their families, I have found that one informal trip to the home can be worth the informational yield of a dozen office visits. The professional will also often need dependable sources of referral for community services: vocational, educational, legal, housing, and others. Finally, at his disposal he requires a living arrangement where he can domicile clients when appropriate, a place that is supportive of sanity and personal reconstruction.

What shall we call this combination detective, guide, social worker, and concierge? The most suitable extant term I have found is *psychological counselor*. Many of my colleagues will frown; in fact, there is an ongoing struggle at all levels on the part of those who call themselves clinical psychologists to limit those who call themselves counselling psychologists from encroaching on the more serious, "medical-type" human problems. People who acquire doctoral degrees will wish, after all, to be recognized as doctors.

More about the role of the professional in the following chapter.

PSYCHIATRY IN THE PRIVATE SECTOR:
Paying Customers Aren't Called Names

MENTAL HEALTH FOR THE RICH AND POOR

Mental hospitals are mainly public institutions and their clientele come mostly from the lower socioeconomic classes. For the more affluent, there is another branch of the mental-health professions: private psychotherapy. The two branches have divergent histories, philosophies, and practices, with some, but not much, overlap. Institutionalized mental patients may receive psychotherapy, but sparingly. The modal treatments are drugs, shock therapies, and something called "milieu therapy" which, in my experience, could range from participation in a mock ward government to daily, arranged interactions with student nurses or volunteers. Private psychotherapy patients may have drugs prescribed for them, but, again, sparingly. Individuals in private psychotherapy are rarely tagged with diagnostic labels, in fact, they are as likely to be called "clients" as "patients." Based on these data, the argument has been lodged that the poor are more prone to serious mental illness than the rich.[1]

DOWN "PSYCHIATRISTS ROW"

Private psychotherapy patients generally find their doctors in the same manner as they find other specialists, medical or otherwise: through family physicians, friends, local medical or psychological associations, or the classified telephone directory. If the latter source is used, particularly in cities, it will probably be noted that psychotherapists' offices, like many other professionals, tend to form a geographic cluster, sometimes called "Psychiatrists Row." In New York City, Psychiatrists Row is the upper 80s between Park and Fifth Avenues; in Toronto it is St. Clair, east of Avenue Road; in Buffalo it is Delaware, north of Bryant.

Here, however, the similarities end. For other medical specialties or specialities in any area – law, accounting, automotive mechanics – the client can usually feel confident that one professional will pursue his problem in the same general manner as another. For psychotherapy, the individual can safely assume that any two given professionals will approach his case in divergent and often antithetical ways.

The literal definition of psychotherapy is "treatment of the psyche." Webster's calls it, "treatment of mental or emotional disorders by psychological means." [2] In customary practice, it consists mainly of conversations between the professional and client, conducted during specified, fifty-minute periods, though in some methods, such as hypnotherapy, conversations are supplemented by more concrete manipulations of various kinds. The contents, styles, and goals of these conversations, however, are as diverse among mental-health professionals as among random passersby on any corner, and the supplemental procedures are equally as heterogeneous.

How many systems of psychotherapy are there? A 1959 book by Robert Harper described thirty-six, which he referred to as "the main types." [3] His 1975 sequel, entitled *The New Psychotherapies*, listed an additional seventeen on the cover, but included more than these. [4] This is not the complete tale, by any means. Many of those in the Harper books are generic in nature; for example, a psychoanalytically oriented psychotherapist may follow the credo of any of a host of individuals, such as Adler, Jung, Rank, Erikson, Horney, or Sullivan. The same applies to such labels as gestalt therapy, existential analysis, conjoint family therapy, or encounter therapy. There are, as well, a variety of lesser-publicized methods. One can only conjecture the total number of divergent therapies in use, but it is certainly in excess of a hundred.

Is there any order in this conglomerate? For example, are different systems associated with different educational backgrounds and academic credentials of professionals? Not at all. M.D.'s and Ph.D.'s are as likely to be in one camp as another.

Are different therapies deemed appropriate for different problems? To a very limited extent – for example, family therapy necessarily requires that the problem involve a family – but in general, each system is based on its author's unique concept of the human personality and applies to the gamut of emotional and behavioral difficulties.

Is there a core of conservative, respected therapies, in contrast to a more radical fringe group? Perhaps most professionals are disdainful of the more libertine movements – like nude encounter groups – or the more frivolous – like computer therapy (which consists, in fact, of talking with a computer). On the other hand, some of the most prominent figures in the field are responsible for some of the most exotic systems; for example, Arthur Janov's primal therapy trains the client to emit blood-curdling screams; Alexander Lowen's bio-energetics involves such activities as kicking a couch. Further, inasmuch as the proponents of each system perceive theirs as the ultimate truth, they tend to view most of the others as ultimate untruths. Albert Ellis, the founder of rational-emotive therapy, has said that those who practice psychoanalysis "are either fools or mentally disturbed."[5] Arguments among therapists are usually more subtly put, but, nonetheless, as definitive.

Thus, a foray into Psychiatrists Row, by whatever means the person gets there, will have the most unpredictable consequences. He may find himself heels up on a couch and free-associating, or screaming in a solitary room, or play-acting scenarios of his life, or analyzing his semantic structure, or rehashing childhood insecurities, or trying to force himself into a circle of others with their arms locked. The following contrasts several of the more common consequences.

If there is a couch in the room for him to lie on, and he is informed that the therapeutic process requires three to five visits a week for at least two years, then the client has stumbled onto an orthodox psychoanalyst. "Orthodox" means that the theories and methods of Freud are followed to the letter. There will be much interpretation of the unconscious significance of verbalizations, attitudes toward the analyst, and dreams, for example, in terms of repressed childhood conflicts revolving around the themes of sex and aggression.

On the other hand, the client may encounter a psychoanalytically oriented psychotherapist, a representative of one of the numerous disciples of Freud who differed in some significant way. The couch will probably be missing and the prescribed number of visits per week and duration of therapy will be markedly less. Most of these therapists will engage, also, in interpretations of present feelings and behavior as unconscious expressions of childhood conflicts, but the nature of the conflicts and interpretations will vary according to the particular neo-Freudian represented. For example, an Adlerian will focus on present forms of overcompensation for the inherent powerlessness of childhood; a Rankian will probe the "birth trauma" and its effects on dependency needs; a Sullivanian will deal with anxieties stemming from early interpersonal insecurities; an Eriksonian will dwell upon the restraints of the childhood environment in the development of autonomy and initiative.

Some psychotherapy-seekers may discover, however, that any reflections on the past are met with derision by the therapist. They will probably be admonished, in fact, to use only the present tense in their discourse and direct their attention to current feelings and events. They will have undoubtedly walked through the door of a gestalt therapist, where, following the precepts of Fritz Perls, the founder, "nothing exists but the here and now." In further contrast to psychoanalytic types, gestalt therapists do not interpret. They do constantly confront and challenge the client's pretensions and inconsistencies, directly and through various "games," in an attempt to lead him to more valid perspectives. For the gestaltist, when a client invokes the past to explain present problems, he is usually seeking to justify himself and avoid necessary change. Gestalt therapists find all systems based on psychoanalysis to be more harmful than helpful.

Other clients may be astounded to find that their therapist says very little, and nothing at all of any significance. Instead he nods, smiles, uh-huhs a lot, and occasionally repeats or rephrases the clients statements. Direct questions will be answered by other questions: "Do you think I'm really angry at my husband?" "Do *you* think that you are really angry at your husband?" This is client-centered therapy, the innovation of Carl Rogers, who felt that interpretations, confrontations, or directions of any kind represented inappropriate impositions of the therapist's values. The client-centered therapist provides "unqualified positive regard" on the premise that it, in itself, will enable the client to work toward his own resolutions.

A rational-emotive therapist will engage the client in precise analyses of his moment-to-moment thought patterns. Clients of Reichian therapy will find themselves prone, perhaps nude, while the doctor examines and manipulates areas of body tension. In reality therapy, the client is encouraged to feel and express "loving involvement" toward the therapist. Systematic desensitization therapists have their clients visualize anxiety-provoking events while trying to maintain a relaxed state. Experiential therapists play-act fantasies with their clients. Direct decision therapists train clients in decisive action. And so on.

PSYCHOTHERAPIES, SNOWFLAKES, AND ARTWORKS

Does it matter on which door one knocks? Are therapies simply like snowflakes, or do some have more or less worth than others?

The research on this question is voluminous. But, given that the "mental illnesses" that bring clients to therapy encompass virtually every human problem and idiosyncracy, and the things therapists do embrace every form and nuance of interpersonal influence, it is not surprising that the yield from the investigation has been nil. In general, studies have failed to confirm that any system is superior to any other, or even that psychotherapy itself is any more than a placebo.[6] There is, in fact, a system called placebo therapy, based on the assumption that the most critical aspect of what the therapist does is convincing the client that he will improve.[7]

Forms of psychotherapy, however, are not as capriciously determined as snowflakes. They are more akin to artwork; that is, they are largely the products of the configuration of needs, personalities, and values of their innovators. A film called *Three Approaches to Psychotherapy*, popular in classrooms for more than two decades, shows Carl Rogers, Fritz Perls, and Albert Ellis each applying his own system with the same patient.[8] One obvious fact is that all perceived the patient and her problem in totally different ways. Another is that each was committed to his system by considerations that were more personal than academic. Rogers, laconic and reserved, with a midwesterner's laissez-faire disdain for intrusiveness, sat back and indulged in the smiles, nods and uh-huhs of unqualified acceptance. Perls, an assertive, imposing, emotional European, could scarcely let a gesture or comment go by without provocative confrontation. Ellis, a metropolitan intellectual, was completely engrossed in definitions of logic and illogic. I suspect that professionals choose the systems they follow on much the same, personal grounds, the particulars of their educations notwithstanding.

This is not to imply that the theories and systems are devoid of wisdom. Some, such as Freud and Erikson, contain some of the great wisdom of the ages; others, perhaps less. But most have a valid perspective on some aspect of human personality and dynamics of change. It is not the stuff of fools (with the possible exception of computer therapy and a few others).

The dilemma of so many theories can be resolved in a most simple manner with the word "sometimes" applied both across different clients and to the same client at different times. It is *sometimes* fruitful to probe childhood experiences. It is *sometimes* preferable to stay in the here and now. The client's conflicts may *sometimes* involve sex; *sometimes* aggression; *sometimes* power; *sometimes* security. *Sometimes* it is best to interpret; *sometimes* to challenge; *sometimes* to offer naught but unqualified positive regard. *Sometimes* the professional may profitably analyze the client's modes of thought; *sometimes* teach him optimal strategies of decision making; *sometimes* have him role-play his fantasies; and *sometimes* engage him in relaxation exercises. *Sometimes* it is beneficial to encourage the clients "loving involvement"; *sometimes* it is wiser not to.

DOCTORING VS. COUNSELLING

The professional for all seasons needs to assimilate all of the sources of wisdom, but he needs even more than this. In the previous chapter we suggested that much of what he does requires the curiosity and problem-solving abilities of a good detective to sustain the frustrating search for motives and for means for change. An additional requisite is compassion: the capacity to feel the needs and emotions of the client so that he can sense when to do what: when to intrude and when to lay back; when to lead and when to follow; when to appeal to reason and when to emotion.

Ultimately, however, his personality will be the dominant force in whatever he does and how successful he is at it. Psychotherapy systems implicitly regard the professional's personality as extraneous, something to be left outside of the therapy room. But it cannot, and should not be. In the interpersonal interaction called psychotherapy, as in any interpersonal interaction, one person will not respond from the deeper recesses of his thoughts, feelings, and values unless he perceives that the other is as well. I have found that the most effective response that I can make to a client, to engender his trust and meaningful communication, is to share with him some of my own past or present problems that relate to his. If the professional tries to exclude his own persona from the process, if he adopts a "therapeutic mien" – aloof, uninvolved, private, non-reciprocal – he will rapidly lose his client's attention, just as he would anyone he engaged in this sort of pseudoencounter.

The professional is greatly benefitted by a comprehensive, formal education in psychological theories and data. He will profit, as well, from exposure to the wide range of approaches of other professionals. The most critical determinant of success, however, resides in the interaction of personalities between his client and himself.

But psycho*therapy* is defined as treatment, and treatment implies fixed, concrete, impersonal methods. The profession that we have described is based on the premise that much of its effectiveness depends on intrinsic human qualities rather than principles acquired from textbooks. Its modus operandi is mainly flying-by-the-seat-of-the-pants. There are no rules, no prescribed procedures for given situations. The only valid term for it is "counselling."

We should not feel diminished by relinquishing our doctor roles for counselor roles. Psychotherapists have an easier time of it than psychological counselors. Just as a physician is held blameless if his patient does not respond to appropriate treatment, in the quasimedical model of psychotherapy, only the client can fail.

But failure in counselling, based as it is on the compatability of both parties, is a shared failure.

All of this may appear to suggest that some persons are better suited than others by temperament and personality to be psychological counselors. This is the implicit and, often, explicit, assumption of most training programs, although the criteria for suitability naturally differ with the program's orientation. If one is deemed a good candidate to practice Rogerian counselling, he probably couldn't get near a Gestalt program.

We have described why curiosity and compassion are necessary qualities, and intelligence goes without saying. Beyond these attributes, however, there is room for widely disparate sorts in the field, for the simple reason that client's problems and personalities are also widely disparate. Counselors are human, and their curiosities and compassions will be directed and circumscribed by their own inescapable natures. Thus, Freud got along well with patients who were reasonably coherent and communicative, but did not relate to the bizarre types characterized as "schizophrenic," and concluded that they were poor prospects for psychoanalysis.[9] One of his most eminent disciples, however, Harry Stack Sullivan, counselled the latter type almost exclusively, but always remained somewhat befuddled about and disdainful toward people who were mainly depressed.[10]

EDUCATING THE CONSUMER

As it is presently constituted, the field cannot acknowledge or follow the basic dictums that compatability of professional and client is a prime requisite for successful counselling. It is constrained by the medical model within which it functions, where credentials are the sole criteria for expertise.

I have suggested in several places that most of the public are probably less naive about the true nature of the mental-health professions than they appear. Nevertheless, many are not, and many are sufficiently ambivalent that when they find themselves in emotional difficulties, they tend to renew their faith in the experts. Thus, until the medical model is shed, a large proportion of clients will continue to find and assess their counselors as they would physicians, and herein, perhaps, is the most odious abuse of the consumer. The client who does not experience positive change will naturally assume, as will the medical patient, that his state of illness is such that he is beyond treatment. I have encountered many individuals, mired in months or even years of stagnant counselling, who replied to my question of why they didn't find another professional with some reference to the credentials or reputations of their doctors.

One step toward educating the consumer was taken by the State of Florida in 1979, when it declined to renew its licensing law for psychologists. A licensing law of any kind implies that there is a specific set of skills and accepted procedures inherent in the activity under license. We license nurses, chiropractors, accountants, and electricians. If there is not a specific set of skills and procedures, however, the licensing law becomes a fraud in itself, for the consumer is misdirected and lulled into suspending his own judgmental capacities.[11]

Most of the public is justifiably confused about the various orders of professionals who practice psychotherapy. Generally it is assumed that psychiatrists offer the highest quality product, by virtue of their M.D. degrees, their higher fees, and the fact that these fees are more readily defrayed by health insurance benefits. Folks that I have talked to are usually surprised to learn that there are no basic differences between psychiatrists and psychologists in terms of what they do, and that the only advantage of seeking the former, aside from insurance coverage, is that he can prescribe chemical euphorics if you desire them, rather than having to refer you to your family physician for this purpose. If asked for a preference, I reply that, all things constant, I lean toward psychologists for two reasons. The ranks of psychiatrists contain a significant number who pursued traditional medical careers for all of the wrong reasons, and turned to psychiatry when they realized that they really didn't want to peer into body orifices or the like for the rest of their lives. They tend to be very poorly motivated and suited for their tasks. Further, the graduate education of the psychologist is considerably more focussed on the developmental and personality theories relevant to counselling. There are talented and untalented in both groups, however, and, for both, the bulk of their formal training encompasses irrelevancies: general medicine in the case of psychiatrists; philosophy of science and research methodology for Ph.D.-level psychologists. I view favorably the movement in some quarters for separate graduate programs for psychologists planning applied careers, to the extent that such programs abandon the medical, in favor of the counselling, model.

To compound the consumer's confusion, "marital counselors" and "family therapists," usually from the fields of social work and education, are separately licensed in many locales. Then there are various other titles, outside the aegis of government regulation, describing healers of emotional ills: psychosynthesists, rolfers, biofeedback trainers, est leaders, pastoral counselors, transcendental meditation teachers, yoga masters, and more.

A total governmental deregulation of the psychological counselling industry would be an important first step toward creating an educated consumer. Let each dispenser present his services, credentials, and fees, and caveat emptor. Consumers who are encouraged to decide for themselves may serve, in turn, to educate the profession about the nature and value of its product.

AFTER THE FALL:
Living Without Mental Illness

A PORTABLE CULTURE

David Saunders and I conducted some demographic research in the late 1970s that revealed that following a mental hospital opening, the mental hospitalization rates for residents of the surrounding area regularly and sharply increased by as much as 400 percent.[1] The result of this increase was that there were differences as high as ten-fold in mental hospital admission rates for residents of neighboring communities, attributable almost exclusively to the location of the nearest institution.

Of course, one possible interpretation is that the nearby presence of a psychiatric hospital has an educative effect on both the public and the general medical community that increases the probability of detection and proper care for mental disease. On this basis, the relationships described above might be found, to some extent, for any medical specialty. The question, however, is whether increased detection can plausibly result in 400 percent increases and ten-fold differences. We reasoned that if it did, we would have to presume vast amounts of untreated, severe mental illness in areas devoid of the influence of a nearby hospital.

Thus we compared areas on every measure we could obtain that might reflect large numbers of seriously mentally ill people, loose in the community. These included rates for divorce, suicide, child abuse, automobile accident fatalities, homocide, assault, sex-related and drug-related offenses. None of these variables showed differences related to the presence of a mental hospital in the area or the mental hospitalization rates of residents.

Our conclusion was that the effect of a nearby psychiatric facility is on the perception, rather than the detection of mental illness. For the people who live within its influence, emotional liabilities or crises, responses to stress, idiosyncracies, adjustment difficulties, interpersonal conflicts, or transgressions of custom on the part of themselves or others cease to be regarded as just these things and become potential signs of mental illness. The mental-health establishment thereby creates its own culture, wherever it lands. And when the culture is in place, people no longer look to themselves for resolutions of the ordinary and extraordinary problems of living. Medical problems are, after all, the province of the medical profession.

THE PSYCHIATRIZATION OF PUBLIC POLICY

Thus, if the Tower of Babel fell, the targets of the mental-health establishment would generally do well enough without it. Society-at-large, however, would be somewhat discomforted. Throughout its existence in this century, psychiatry has progressively and tenaciously increased its role in public policy. Most people are probably aware from the media about such matters as civil commitment and the insanity defense, but unaware, unless they have been touched directly, of the multitude of other possible incursions of psychiatry in their lives.[2]

Mental-health professionals routinely assess individuals for "mental illness" at the behest of courts or other governmental agencies, in regard to such decisions as granting of abortions; parental custody of children; employment in certain public occupations; enlistment in or discharge from the military; removal of children from the regular educational system; suitability of prospective adoptive parents or children for adoption; and the right to manage one's own assets. Even after death, a psychiatrist may be called upon to determine whether the person was "of sound mind" when he made out his will. If an individual is arrested, no matter what the charge or circumstance, he may be subjected to a psychiatric examination to establish whether or not he has a mental illness that could render him incompetent to properly assist his attorney. If it is so determined, he will remain in a mental institution until psychiatrists find him competent, and then come to trial. Mental-health professionals are also invited, in most jurisdictions, to play some role in determining the outcomes of convictions. In California, all convicted sex offenders appear before a psychiatrist and, if declared ill, spend an indefinite term in a mental hospital before beginning their sentences. It is pro forma in Texas for psychiatrists to testify, in sentencing hearings involving violent crimes, in regard to the convicted party's propensity for further behavior of this kind. One professional so frequently moved juries to maximum sentences by his definitive, intimidating pronouncements that he was dubbed "Dr. Death" by defense attorneys and was even disavowed by his peers.[3]

THE INSANITY DEFENSE: WHY HINCKLEY MADE IT AND HEARST DIDN'T

If the reader has accepted the thesis of this book thus far, it is apparent that in all of these capacities, as in every other endeavor we have discussed, there are no objective standards for psychiatric opinions: they are based on personal values, whims, and circumstances of the moment. In some areas, the process borders on the absurd. For example, no one who follows the news will fail to realize that, in any case involving the insanity defense, attorneys can acquire all the psychiatric experts they need to testify on both sides of the issue. One research question that I have tried in vain to answer is: How often do psychiatrists turn down the defense or prosecuting attorneys who solicited them on the grounds that their expert opinion will not support the attorney's case? If defendants were examined objectively, this should happen about half of the time for defense and prosecuting attorneys combined. My suspicion, however, confirmed by three of 24 attorneys approached by my interviewers who replied directly to the question, is that the actual answer is close to never.

There is one way, however, in which the insanity defense is very much unlike other interactions between psychiatry and the law: it is not customarily used to limit individual rights or liberties. In contrast, it allows judges and juries to avoid convictions in cases where there are mitigating circumstances – which are not regarded as such by the law – but nevertheless evoke their sympathies. Recent, publicized, successful cases, for example, include an unemployed man who surreptitiously absconded with a large sum of money that had fallen from an armored truck in a traffic accident[4] and a woman who murdered her husband in retaliation for "sexual humiliations."[5] There was a time when the phrase "The Unwritten Law" referred to the use of the insanity defense on behalf of cuckolded husbands who did in their wives and/or rivals. As male-oriented, moral codes give way to feminism, the new unwritten law may pertain to wives who eliminate abusive mates.

If jurors gave serious attention to the testimony of psychiatrists, most insanity pleas would succeed, rather than the small proportion that actually do. Juries are instructed that if they find "reasonable doubt" that the defendant is *sane*, they must bring in a verdict of not guilty. No rational layperson could *not* be beset by "reasonable doubt" when confronted with the homogeneous testimony of a battery of medical experts, unless that person totally disregards the experts' supposed expertise. For example, after Patty Hearst was convicted, despite the presence of a veritable *Who's Who* of mental health for the defense, one juror commented to a television newsman that most of the jurors felt that the doctors didn't know any more than they did.

The "implicit pact" among judges, juries, and the public in regard to psychiatric testimony is that it is to be used or not by jurors as their sympathies with the case dictate. The trial of John Hinckley, Jr. was the exception that highlighted this rule. His jury, for whatever reason, accepted its mandate literally. With professed reluctance, they naively but logically assumed that agreement by a number of eminent physicians must constitute reasonable doubt, and, to the dismay and confusion of many, including the judge who had instructed them, they acquitted the would-be assassin of President Ronald Reagan.

A TWO-EDGED SWORD

As a bit of duplicity by which the law is tempered in the defendant's favor when common sentiment so dictates, the insanity defense represents a violation of truth and medical integrity, but because of the way it is used, it may not provoke the sensibilities of the democratic idealist. For every individual who eludes punishment by the insanity plea, however, there are literally hundreds who are over-sentenced by virtue of other machinations of mental-health professionals in the criminal courts. It is a two-edged sword, but the sharper edge is pointed toward the defendant.

The most common device of this nature regards the concept of "competency to stand trial." Intelligence is a variable attribute among homo sapiens. Except for rare cases of profound feeble-mindedness, however, people who have been arrested are capable of understanding the nature and possible consequences of the charges against them at a level where they can respond appropriately to their attorney's questions. Forensic psychiatric institutions, however, are mainly populated by persons remanded there indefinitely, prior to trial, because they have been found "incompetent" in these regards.[6] We should expect these places to be great repositories for blithering idiots, but most of the residents of the institutions I have visited can engage you in reasonable conversations about the institutional food, yesterday's football game, their lives, or whatever.

Incompetent defendants, then, serve their psychiatric sentences plus their legal sentences. The procedure is generally invoked when the individual's demeanor, history, or alleged offense is such that common sympathy would probably favor punishment in excess of what the law would customarily allow.[7] In my experience, sex offenders are prime candidates (except in jurisdictions, like California, where there is separate legislation to provide the means for indefinite terms in mental institutions). So, too, are child and wife abusers, and, often, those who have strained the patience of the court by repeated, minor, nuisance offenses, like drunk and disorderly charges. Indifference, surliness, or any indication of nonrepentance may readily qualify the defendant for a competency assessment, as will prior contact with the mental-health professions, if this comes to the attention of the judge or prosecuting attorney. Not surprisingly, defense attorneys almost never move for such assessments, although they are in the best position to judge whether their clients are capable of assisting them.

Abuses in the name of competency to stand trial sometimes defy belief. Among recent cases brought to light is one involving a man, accused of attempted purse-snatching, who was held for sixteen years, and another involving a man alleged to have burglarized a railroad car, who was confined for thirty-five.[8] In an attempt to minimize such atrocities, the United States Supreme Court in 1972 decreed that if, "after a reasonable period of time," a professional prediction cannot be made that an incompetent defendant will attain competency "in the foreseeable future," he must be released or undergo civil commitment proceedings.[9] It is doubtful that such generalities will have much affect, particularly in view of the fact, which we will discuss below, that examiners can usually, readily find grounds for civil commitment if they are so inclined. Moreover, even if we could assure that defendants are not detained more than a year or so beyond their legal sentences, rather than sixteen or thirty-five, would this really represent a victory for Constitutional rights? Practices that are inherently corrupt do not lend themselves to reform; there are no means to render them righteous.

MENTAL-HEALTH STATUTES:
THE CASE FOR ABOLITION

The 1970s have also seen attempts at reform of civil commitment procedures. Many states and provinces in North America amended their mental-health statutes in the direction of narrowing the professional's options, generally requiring more precisely stated reasons for commitments and more frequent reviews of involuntary patients.

Again, I do not foresee that such measures will be significant deterrents to business-as-usual. In fact, Michael Bagby and I found that in the Province of Ontario, proportions of mental-hospital admissions that were involuntary actually increased following revised legislation, and similar findings have been reported for the State of California.[10]

It has been well documented, and publicly acknowledged by no less a personage than the president of the American Psychiatric Association, that *there are no valid or even generally accepted criteria to predict an individual's potential for harm to himself or others*, which are the universal grounds for civil commitment.[11] Thus, in the absence of concrete criteria, an examiner can appear to be as precise as the state requires about anyone. Rather than scribbling "suicidal tendencies" or "explosive type," as in the pre-reform days, he may describe an allegation, no matter how dubious, of a threat the examinee, supposedly made, or talk about suicidal signs in projective test responses.

In regard to more frequent reviews of involuntary patients, there is no reason to expect that scheduling changes will make these less a folly than described in Chapter 4.

But the larger question is whether reform, effective or not, is an appropriate approach to civil commitments. The principle of due process of law represents the hard-earned progress of civilization toward a balance between public welfare and individual rights. Any time an individual is denied due process—interned without charge, sentenced without trial—the entire fabric of free society is compromised. Democracy cannot exist without the principle of due process; mental-health statutes cannot exist with it. What is required is abolition.

There is a reluctance toward abolition, even among those who are enlightened about both the foibles of psychiatry and the sanctity of due process. The question is usually put: Shall we allow people who appear injurious to themselves or to others to remain unfettered until they commit some tragic act? The question, however, begs the issue. The revocation of psychiatric powers will not necessarily lead to a more or less permissive standard of behavior. It will require that legislative and judicial bodies take their rightful roles in filling voids in the application of common law that have been concealed for many decades by civil commitment procedures.

The law is not so limited as to render its agencies incapable of preventive action. If a police officer finds someone threatening another with a club, he does not wait until the blow is landed before intervening. Suicide attempts are actionable offenses in every jurisdiction, on a number of grounds. Criminal code categories such as endangerment, public nuisance, assault, and disorderly conduct can be applied to anyone who appears potentially harmful to himself or others.

Why, then, do we invest doctors with the combined authority of police, jury, judge, and parole officer, and abide a system that routinely deprives citizens of their most basic constitutional rights?

One reason frequently given is that psychiatry can provide the best available resolution of the legal and moral dilemmas inherent in highly ambiguous cases. Many people I have spoken with, including those at all levels of law enforcement, were not misled about the tenuousness of psychiatric judgments but believed that mental-health professionals were, nevertheless, capable of the most learned decisions possible.

In my own direct experience, however, I observed that, not only were professionals' decisions based on personal values, but these were as heterogeneous among them as any nonprofessional group. I worked alongside one who routinely institutionalized anyone who had made a suicidal gesture, preferring to err on the side of caution; I worked with another who routinely turned them loose, regarding them as harmless attention-seekers. I have encountered a teetotaller who needed no other justification than intoxication to convince him of someone's dangerousness; a feminist with a vigilant eye for potential wife-abusers who certified, pro forma, the male parties of domestic brawls; and her male counterpart who perceived potentially self-destructive "hysterical personality disorders" in most emotionally distraught women who were referred to him.

If the truth be known, the actual decisions about dangerousness are generally made before the mental-health professional is called. Law officers are aware of the fact that hospital staffs cannot protect themselves or the community against truly destructive persons, so these are kept in jail; this provides some explanation for the seeming paradox that the crime rate for former mental patients is lower than for the population-at-large.[12]

A second rationale for civil commitments in lieu of criminal charges is that the penal system is inappropriate for those interned in psychiatric hospitals. Critics, in fact, will suggest that I am advocating a return to a more primitive age, when the mentally disturbed were dealt with as common criminals.

It should first be pointed out that convicted criminals are favored in many regards; for example, fixed sentences, specified conditions for appeal and parole, and the right not to participate in chemical experiments (see Chapter 4). In principle and in practice, individuals under detention fare better in places clearly defined as penal institutions, where confinement is penalty for some act that is deemed intolerable to society and thereby illegal. The compromise of both human dignity and human rights customarily begins when individual liberties are withheld in the name of the person's "own good." This is how Nazis explained Jewish ghettos in 1933; how plantation owners in the southern United States justified black slavery in the nineteenth century; how the totalitarian regime in Poland rationalizes the recent imposition of martial law. The term "penalty" linguistically and legally implies a prescribed, limited action; however, there are no bounds to what may be imposed upon a person "for his own good." Thus, recent cases include a New York City woman committed for sixteen years following an incident of public intoxication; a Pennsylvania man held for thirty-two years based on a disturbance of the peace during a domestic encounter; and a sixty-seven-year-old man in Saskatchewan, Canada, who is still confined for putting a rock on a railroad track when a teenager.[13]

There are no inherent limitations, however, of the varieties of penal institutions that may be established. The limitations are mainly economic, and the mental hospital happens to be a very expensive variety: between two and three hundred dollars per day per inmate, in most locales. The public revenues spared by divesting the field of medicine of its penal functions will go a long way toward creating whatever sorts of sanctuaries are deemed appropriate. The model may be the retreat, or the half-way house, or the original Quaker farm (a brief, benevolent, nineteenth-century innovation, quickly usurped by the psychiatric establishment). Psychological counsellors, as we have defined the role in Chapter 8, may certainly make a contribution in these places, but solely at the behest of – while being responsible to – their clients.

Mental-health statutes, then, are unnecessary for the protection of society or the individuals who are committed, but these are not really the reasons why they endure. The reason is that it is in the interests of the prevailing social class to keep ambiguous acts outside of the criminal code. We have noted that the victims of civil commitments are, overwhelmingly, the poor and uneducated. Economically favored persons, as well, undergo emotional crises that evoke suicidal gestures, threats to others, and all forms of untoward and unusual behaviors. But just as the inquisitors focussed their attentions away from the nobility – except in rare cases when sanctioned by even more powerful nobility – so too is psychiatric law highly selective; it does not ordinarily bite the hands that sustain it. Thus there is a dual legal standard. Those among the lower socioeconomic strata who appear to be a danger or nuisance can be expeditiously disposed of without requiring judicial precedents that might ultimately compromise the licenses and liberties of the advantaged.

It follows that repeal of mental-health laws will herald a period of societal self-revelation. Legal definitions and specifications will have to be developed, based on community standards, for the tenuous cases we now delegate to doctors. We will have to deal directly with such questions as whether suicide attempters should be charged and detained; what the conditions shall be for criminal actions in domestic altercations; what sorts of atypical behavior will be cause for legal restraint. The yields, however, are no less than the restoration of truth, both in medical science and public policy, and equality under the law.

CHILD ABUSE, PROFESSIONAL STYLE

A consideration of psychiatry's public mandate needs to give special attention to its role with children, because it is so pervasive and because there are special considerations and consequences inherent in any institutional abuse of the very young.

We have discussed the ideological functions of the mental-health professions in the educational system: the isolation of academically slower children through use of the category "cultural-familial retardation"; the chemical control of rambunctious or rebellious children by labelling them "hyperkinetic." But the net is much wider. Whenever a problem involving a child comes to the attention of a public agency, whether it is by virtue of the child's behavior or circumstance, the likelihood is that he will, sooner or later, undergo a mental-health assessment. And whenever anyone, child or adult, is subject to a mental-health assessment, the likelihood is that he will emerge with a psychiatric label.

It is not that social workers and others in the front lines of crisis intervention with children are particularly taken in by clinical jargon. Most that I have known seemed skeptical of the reports of psychiatric and clinical-psychological "experts," in part because the experts generally see the child very briefly and in a limited context, whereas the front-line case workers have probably dealt intensely with the child and the significant people in his life, family, teachers, etc., for months or longer.

Front-line workers, however, usually succumb to pressures at all levels to seek and abide by the counsel of the experts, for the implication is that not to do so is tantamount to practicing medicine without a license.

Public revenues for children are substantial, and the windfall they provide the mental-health professions is responsible for some fierce territorial squabbles. These not only occur between doctors and case workers, but between the two doctor-level specialties: psychology and psychiatry. The American Psychological Association refused for a year to give formal sanction to the 1980 revised diagnostic manual, developed for use by all professionals by the American Psychiatric Association. The psychologists felt that the plethora of new diagnostic categories for children and adolescents in the revision reflected the intentions of the M.D.'s to move psychologists out of the field.[14]

Unfortunately, no matter who wins this battle, the losers are the children. More than anything else, my experiences as consultant to child-care agencies determined my decision to write this dissent. The children I encountered were virtually always victims of untoward family situations but had nevertheless received some opprobrious psychiatric brand. Agencies, after all, would probably not suffer their fees for long if the doctors did not find illness. Social workers deal with deficiencies in the home much less expensively. Thus, an interview of an hour or so by a doctor, with much of this time used for the child to draw pictures or invent stories, customarily yielded labels like "childhood schizophrenia," "autism," "hyperkinesis," "minimal brain dysfunction," or "asocial personality disorder."

I spent most of my energy disclaiming these stigmata and trying to dispel their consequences to the children, which ranged from isolation in school to protracted drugging and/or institutionalization. In the process, I became enormously impressed with the malleability of the young: their responsiveness to the transition from dehumanizing influences to loving, supportive, nonjudgmental adult care. It is not very difficult to provide. The best examples I found, other than quality foster or adoptive parenting, were in group homes administered by people with affinities and affections for children and sufficient astuteness to realize that these qualities were not embodied by the writers of psychiatric diagnostic manuals. Again, the monies used for institutional child psychiatry could provide sufficient numbers of such places to serve all children in need, with change to spare.

SMOKING, STAGEFRIGHT, AND THIRTY-TWO OTHER NEW ILLNESSES: THE EMPEROR DENUDED

I have no doubt that, as were its forebears, the concept of mental illness will eventually be retired to the archives of malevolent mythology. It is futile, however, to try to predict how and when. The police powers of the inquisitions sustained the search for demonic possession for some 500 years, and it was only after the separation of the church from the affairs of state that that notion began to dissipate. It may be that the mental-illness myth derives much of its legitimacy, as well, from the legal and quasi-legal functions of mental-health professionals, and its repudiation will require their disengagement from public policy at all levels. To the extent that this is so, it foretells an arduous process, for the benefactors of the ideology, who compose the prevailing social powers, will not readily relinquish their advantages.

Historically, however, there has been a tendency for the self-destruction of oppressive ideologies by their own avarice, and this may be happening within psychiatry today.

The 1980, revised *Diagnostic and Statistical Manual* of the American Psychiatric Association (D.S.M. III) is about four times the length of its predecessor.[15] In addition to elaborations of extant diagnostic categories, creating two or more out of one, it presents *34 brand new psychiatric illnesses*.[16] Other medical specialities labor to eliminate illnesses; psychiatrists manufacture them.

Why the sudden expansion? There is no point in searching for even a quasilegitimate reason. Professionals had not thought nor heard of these illnesses before D.S.M. III; that is, their appearance in the revision could not have been anticipated except by the writers. Psychologists, as mentioned earlier, perceived it as an attempt to usurp their position. This may have been a partial factor, but I believe there was a more basic motive.

In the United States during the last half of the 1970s, the establishment of a national health insurance program appeared inevitable; the only issue that seemed to remain was whether it would be President Carter's or Senator Kennedy's version. Psychiatrists have learned from hard experience that insurance underwriters have a more parsimonious approach to the concept of illness than psychiatrists do; in fact, the profession has had to lobby assiduously for the restricted benefits it does receive from various state and private plans. Thus, it is quite feasible that the hidden agenda for the expanded Manual was: The more diseases there are to negotiate about in the federal program to come, the more profitable the outcome.

This is quite obvious in some additions. *Tobacco Dependence* (Category number 305.1), for example, opens the door for benefits to a vast segment of the population. *Ego-dystonic Homosexuality* (302.00) replaced just plain old homosexuality, which, as noted in Chapter 4, was voted out of D.S.M. II. The new category is reserved for those with "persistent concern," which means that a homosexual is ill only if he is ambivalent about his sexual activities. This may not make sense medically, but it does from an insurance standpoint, inasmuch as these are the only ones who would seek aid. Similarly, problems with "The Big O" now constitute illness (302.73: *Inhibited Female Orgasm*), undoubtedly inspired by the possibility of coverage for the many sex "clinics" and "therapies" that have appeared in the last decade.

As indicated earlier, there are a host of new illnesses for children and adolescents. *Conduct Disorder* is one, and it comes in four possible combinations depending on whether the subject is socialized or not, and aggressive or not. From the examples in the Manual, a child with friends who fights would be *Conduct Disorder, Socialized, Aggressive* (312.23); one without friends who lies would be *Conduct Disorder, Undersocialized, Nonaggressive* (312.10). One with friends who lies would be, naturally, *Conduct Disorder, Socialized, Nonaggressive* (312.21). If the child doesn't do anything particularly upsetting, but is generally negativistic to authority, he suffers a different, new illness called *Oppositional Disorder* (313.81).

Adults get their due, as well. There are a number of interesting new "personality disorders", including *Avoidant Personality Disorder* (301.82), characterized by "hypersensitivity to potential rejection, humiliation, or shame"; *Borderline Personality Disorder* (310.83), which features "instability in a variety of areas, including interpersonal behavior, mood, and self-image"; and *Dependent Personality Disorder* (301.60), in which one "passively allows others to assume responsibility for major areas of his or her life." There is *Intermittant Explosive Disorder* (312.24), referring to occasional losses of temper, whereas *Isolated Explosive Disorder* (312.35) refers to one big one. Stagefright is now a disease, *Social Phobia* (300.23), the fear of being exposed to "scrutiny by others," such as when "speaking or performing in public." First prize for self-parody, however, goes to *Factitious Disorder with Psychological Symptoms* (300.16), which is the mental illness that describes individuals who pretend to be mentally ill.

As it turned out, the political climate changed suddenly in 1980, and national health insurance does not seem to be a viable possibility, at least for the near future. Regardless, the profession may have hoisted itself on its own petard. The esoteric, ambiguous labels of psychiatry are the Emperor's Clothes. Even if people do not fully believe them, they justify acceptance of the ideology, and pacification of the collective conscience. The confessions of D.S.M. III, confirming unabashedly how psychiatrists *really* think about illness, may take the public past its own tolerance for self-delusion.

It is a small hope.

NOTES

CHAPTER 1

1. Brill, H. "Nosology," in A. M. Freedman and H. I. Kaplan (eds.), *Comprehensive Textbook of Psychiatry* (Baltimore: Williams & Wilkins, 1967), p. 581.
2. Pierce, C. M., Mathis, J. L., and Pishkin, V. "Basic psychiatry in twelve hours," *Diseases of the Nervous System* 29 (1968): pp. 533–535.
3. Scheff, T. J. "The societal reaction to deviance: Ascriptive elements on the psychiatric screening of mental patients in a midwestern state," *Social Problems* 11 (1964): pp. 401–413.
4. Temberlin, M. K. "Diagnostic bias in community mental health," *Community Mental Health Journal* 6 (1970): pp. 108–118.
5. Rosenhan, D. L. "On being sane in insane places," *Science* 179 (1973): pp. 250–257.
6. Szasz, T. S. (ed.). *The Age of Madness* (New York: Aronson, 1974), pp. 167–170.
7. Srole, L., Langer, T. S., Michael, S. T., Opler, M. K., and Rennie, T. A. C. *Mental Health in the Metropolis: The Midtown Manhattan Study* (New York: McGraw-Hill, 1962).

CHAPTER 2

1. *Mental Illness: Fact or Myth? The Szasz-Ellis Debate*, videotape produced by William E. Simon (Baldwin, N.Y., 1977).
2. Schrag, P. and Divocky, D. *The Myth of the Hyperactive Child* (New York: Dell, 1975).
3. Braginsky, D. and Braginsky, B. M. *Hansels and Gretels: Studies of Children in Institutions for the Mentally Retarded* (New York: Holt, Rinehart & Winston, 1971).
4. Gal, P. "Mental disorders of advanced years," *Geriatrics* 14 (1959): pp. 224–228.
5. Shoben, E. J., Jr. "Toward a concept of the normal personality," *American Psychologist* 12 (1957): pp. 183–189.
6. Coleman, J. C. *Abnormal Psychology and Modern Life*, 5th edition (Glenview, Ill.: Scott, Foresman & Co., 1976), p. 15.
7. Bloch, S. and Reddaway, P. *Russia's Political Hospitals* (London: Gollancz, 1977).

CHAPTER 3

1. Szasz, T. S. *The Manufacture of Madness* (New York: Harper & Row, 1970), p. 64.
2. *Toronto Star*, August 22, 1977, p. C3.
3. Szasz, T. S. (ed.). *The Age of Madness* (New York: Aronson, 1974), p. 43.
4. *New York Times*, September 4, 1977, p. 24.
5. Ennis, B. *Prisoners of Psychiatry* (New York: Harcourt, Brace, Jovanovich, 1972).
6. *Toronto Star* (Weekend Magazine Section) May 21, 1977, p. 16.
7. Schrag, P. and Divocky, D. *The Myth of the Hyperactive Child* (New York: Dell, 1975).
8. Ibid. See also Brown, J. L., and Bing, S. R. "Drugging children: Child abuse by professionals," in Koocher, G. P. (ed.), *Children's Rights and the Mental Health Professions* (New York: Wiley, 1976).
9. Walker III, S., "Drugging the American child: We're too cavalier about hyperactivity," *Psychology Today*, December 1974, pp. 43–48.
10. Saunders, D. and Silverman, I. "Extraneous factors in institutionalization for mental retardation: Demographic analyses for Ontario," *Canadian Journal of Community Mental Health* Vol. I (1982): pp. 107–112.
11. Braginsky, D. and Braginsky, B. M. *Hansels and Gretels: Studies of Children in Institutions for the Mentally Retarded* (New York: Holt, Rinehart & Winston, 1971).
12. The category *senile dementia* is independent of the various authentic illnesses, such as cerebral arteriosclerosis, that affect mental processes and are more common in the aged.
13. Staff of C. R. M. Books (eds.). *Abnormal Psychology: Current Perspectives* (Del Mar, Cal.: C. R. M. Books, 1972), p. 180.
14. Broverman, I. K., Broverman, D. M., Clarkson, F. E., Rosenkrantz, P. S., and Vogel, S. R. "Sex-role stereotypes and clinical judgements of mental health," *Journal of Consulting and Clinical Psychology* 34 (1970), pp. 1–7.

CHAPTER 4

1. Szasz, T. S. *The Manufacture of Madness* (New York: Harper & Row, 1970).
2. Zax, M. and Cowan, E. L. *Abnormal Psychology: Changing Conceptions*, 2nd edition (New York: Holt, Rinehart and Winston, 1976), pp. 40–41.
3. Szasz, *The Manufacture of Madness*, p. 65.
4. See, for example, Davison, G. C. and Neale, J. M. *Abnormal Psychology*, 2nd edition (New York: Wiley, 1978), pp. 68–78.
5. Honors Dissertation (1974). Available from the Resource Center of the Psychology Department, York University, Toronto, Ontario, Canada.
6. *Diagnostic and Statistical Manual of Mental Disorders*, 2nd edition (Washington, D.C.: American Psychiatric Association, 1968).

7. Coleman, D. "Who's mentally ill?" *Psychology Today*, January 1978, pp. 34–41.

8. See, for example, Hollingshead, A. B. and Redlich, F. C. *Social Class and Mental Illness: A Community Study* (New York: Wiley, 1958).

9. Foucault, M. *Madness and Civilization* (New York: Vintage, 1965).

10. Szasz, T. S. (ed.). *The Age of Madness* (New York: Aronson, 1974).

11. From Foucault, *Madness and Civilization*, p. 47.

12. Szasz, *The Age of Madness*, pp. 7–8.

13. Foucault, *Madness and Civilization*, p. 40.

14. Szasz, *The Age of Madness*, pp. 20–21.

15. Szasz, *The Manufacture of Madness*, pp. 148–149.

16. Brenner, M. H. *Mental Illness and the Economy* (Cambridge: Harvard University Press, 1973).

17. Foucault, *Madness and Civilization*, p. 40.

18. See, for example, Wright, F. L., Jr. *Out of Sight, Out of Mind* (Philadelphia: National Mental Health Foundation, 1947); Rawls, W. *Cold Storage* (New York: Simon and Schuster, 1980); and articles on abuses in the Southeast Florida State Hospital in the *Miami Herald*, October 5 through 29, 1979.

CHAPTER 5

1. Kraepelin, E. *Dementia Praecox* (New York: Robert E. Krieger, 1971).

2. Kraepelin, E. *Dementia Praecox*, p. 89.

3. Bleuler, E. *Dementia Praecox or the Group of Schizophrenias* (New York: International Universities Press, 1950 [English translation of 1911 publication]).

4. Lehmann, H. E. "Schizophrenia. I: Introduction and history," in A. M. Freedman and H. I. Kaplan (eds.), *Comprehensive Textbook of Psychiatry* (Baltimore: Williams & Wilkins, 1967), p. 596.

5. Bleuler, *Dementia Praecox or the Group of Schizophrenias*, p. 9.

6. Torrey, E. F. "Tracking the causes of madness," *Psychology Today*, March 1979, p. 78.

7. Beck, A. T., Ward, C. H., Mendelson, M., Mock, J. E., and Erbaugh, J. K. "Reliability of psychiatric diagnosis: II. A study of consistency of clinical judgements and ratings," *American Journal of Psychiatry* 119 (1962): pp. 351–357.

8. Weiner, H. "Schizophrenia. III: Etiology," in Freedman and Kaplan (eds.), *Comprehensive Textbook of Psychiatry*, p. 604.

9. Rubins, J. L. "The growth process and schizophrenia: A holistic, psychodynamic approach," in D. V. Siva Sankar (ed.), *Schizophrenia: Current Concepts and Research* (Hicksville, N.Y.: PJD Publications, 1969), p. 1.

10. Bellak, L. and Fielding, C. "Diagnosing schizophrenia," in B. B. Wolman (ed.), *Clinical Diagnosis of Mental Disorders* (New York: Plenum, 1978), p. 757.

11. C.R.M. Books, 1972 (eds.). *Abnormal Psychology: Current Perspectives* (Del Mar, Cal.: C.R.M. Books, 1972), p. 277.

12. Sartorius, N., Shapiro, R., and Jablonsky, A. "The international pilot study of schizophrenia," *Schizophrenia Bulletin* 2 (1974): pp. 21–35.

13. Foucault, M. *Madness and Civilization* (New York: Vintage, 1965), p. 65.

14. *Diagnostic and Statistical Manual of Mental Disorders*, 3rd edition (Washington, D.C.: American Psychiatric Association, 1980), p. 367.

15. Ibid., p. 181.

16. Ibid.

17. See, for example, Rubins, J. L., "The growth process and schizophrenia," p. 1.

18. See Carlsson, A. "Antipsychotic drugs, neurotransmitters, and schizophrenia," *American Journal of Psychiatry* 135 (1978), pp. 164–173.

19. Summarized from L. Bellak and L. Loeb (eds.). *The Schizophrenic Syndrome* (New York: Grune & Stratton, 1969).

20. See Slater, E. and Cowie, V. *The Genetics of Mental Disorder* (London: Oxford University of Press, 1971), p. 97.

21. *Diagnostic and Statistical Manual*, 3rd edition, p. 183.

CHAPTER 6

1. Bakan, D. "Psychology can now kick the science habit," *Psychology Today*, March 1972, p. 88.

2. This tenet has been made explicit in *Diagnostic and Statistical Manual of Mental Disorders*, 3rd edition (Washington, D.C.: American Psychiatric Association, 1980), p. 285.

3. Zax, M. and Cowen, E. L. *Abnormal Psychology: Changing Conceptions*, 2nd edition (New York: Holt, Rinehart and Winston, 1976), pp. 144–145.

4. Szasz, T. S. (ed.). *The Age of Madness* (New York: Aronson, 1974), p. 155.

5. Vonnegut, M. *The Eden Express* (New York: Bantam Books, 1976).

6. Ibid., p. 159.

7. Ibid., p. 161.

8. See Braginsky, B. M., Braginsky, D. D., and Ring, K. *Methods of Madness: The Mental Hospital as a Last Resort* (New York: Holt, Rinehart and Winston, 1969); and Perrucci, R. *Circle of Madness: On Being Insane and Institutionalized in America* (Englewood Cliffs, N.J.: Prentice-Hall, 1974).

CHAPTER 7

1. Freidrich, O. *Going Crazy: An Inquiry into Madness in Our Time* (New York: Avon, 1975), p. 9.

2. See Hoffman, L. *Foundations of Family Therapy* (New York: Basic Books, 1981), pp. 16–36.

3. Seligman, M. E. P. *Helplessness: On Depression, Development and Death* (San Francisco: Freeman, 1975).

4. English, O. S., Hampe, W. W., Jr., Bacon, C. L., and Settlage, C. F.

Direct Analysis and Schizophrenia: Clinical Observations and Evaluations (New York: Grune & Stratton, 1961).

5. Haley, J. *The Power Tactics of Jesus Christ and Other Essays* (New York: Avon, 1969), pp. 9–26.

6. Goffman, E. *Interaction Ritual: Essays on Face-to-Face Behavior* (Chicago: Aldine, 1967), p. 148.

7. Cohen, I. S. (ed.). *Perspectives on Psychology: Introductory Readings* (New York: Praeger, 1975), pp. 389–394.

8. Haley, *The Power Tactics of Jesus Christ and Other Essays*, pp. 145–176.

CHAPTER 8

1. Hollingshead, A. B. and Redlich, F. C. *Social Class and Mental Illness: A Community Study* (New York: Wiley, 1958).

2. Webster's New International Dictionary, 3rd ed., s.v. "psychotherapy."

3. Harper, R. A. *Psychoanalysis and Psychotherapy* (Englewood Cliffs, N.J.: Prentice-Hall, 1959).

4. Harper, R. A. *The New Psychotherapies* (Englewood Cliffs, N.J.: Prentice-Hall, 1975).

5. *Mental Illness: Fact or Myth? The Szasz-Ellis Debate*, videotape produced by William E. Simon (Baldwin, N.Y., 1977).

6. For an overview, see Davison, G. C. and Neale, J. M. *Abnormal Psychology*, 2nd edition (New York: Wiley, 1978): Chaps. 18–20.

7. Harper, *The New Psychotherapies*, p. 154.

8. *Three Approaches to Psychotherapy*, produced by Psychological Films (Santa Ana, California, 1965).

9. Freud, S. *A General Introduction to Psychoanalysis* (New York: Pocket Books, 1924), p. 446.

10. Sullivan, H. S. *Clinical Studies in Psychiatry* (New York: W. W. Norton, 1956), pp. 396–397.

11. After considerable lobbying by the Florida Psychological Association, the law was restored in 1982.

CHAPTER 9

1. Silverman, I. and Saunders, D. "Creating the mental illness culture: Demographic studies of institutionalization in Ontario." *Canadian Psychology* 21 (1980): pp. 121–128.

2. For a complete description, see Robitscher, J. *The Powers of Psychiatry* (Boston: Houghton-Mifflin, 1980).

3. *Time*, June 1, 1981, p. 64.

4. *Toronto Star*, May 7, 1982, p. 1.

5. See, for example, *The Toronto Globe and Mail*, November 20, 1980, p. 4.

6. *Competency to Stand Trial and Mental Illness* (Rockville, Md.: the National Institute of Mental Health, Center for Studies of Crime and Delinquency, 1972).

7. Halpern, A. L. "Use and misuse of psychiatry in competency examinations of criminal defendants," in Bonnie, R. J. (ed.). *Psychiatrists and Legal Process* (New York: Insight Communication, 1977), pp. 102–129.

8. See, respectively, *Toronto Star*, December 22, 1980, p. A1; and Rawls, W. *Cold Storage* (New York: Simon and Schuster, 1980).

9. *Jackson* v. *Indiana*, 406 U.S. 715 (1972).

10. Lamb, H. R., Sorkin, M. A., and Zusman, J. "Legislating social control of the mentally ill in California," *American Journal of Psychiatry* 138 (1981): pp. 334–339.

11. See *Donahue Transcript #02250*, February 25, 1980 (available from Multimedia Program Productions, 140 W. Ninth Street, Cincinnati, Ohio), p. 13.

12. See Shah, S. A. "Dangerousness and civil commitment of the mentally ill: Some public policy considerations," *American Journal of Psychiatry* 132 (1975): pp. 501–505.

13. See, respectively, Ennis, B. *Prisoners of Psychiatry* (New York: Harcourt, Brace, Javanovich, 1972), p. 109; Rawls, *Cold Storage*; and the *Toronto Star*, August 23, 1973, p. A18.

14. *APA Monitor* Washington, D.C.: Newsletter of the *American Psychological Association*, January, 1980), p. 1.

15. *Diagnostic and Statistical Manual of Mental Disorders*, 3rd edition (Washington, D.C.: American Psychiatric Association, 1980).

16. *Diagnostic and Statistical Manual of Mental Disorders*, 2nd edition (Washington, D.C.: American Psychiatric Association, 1968), pp. 371–387.

INDEX

ABOUT THE AUTHOR

Irwin Silverman received a Ph.D. in psychology from the University of Rochester in 1962. He has been on the faculties of the State University of New York at Buffalo and the University of Florida, and is presently at York University in Toronto, Canada. Concurrent with these appointments, he has held a variety of professional service and consultant positions. Professor Silverman has authored more than seventy scholarly publications and presentations encompassing, in addition to the topic of this book, such diverse areas as courtship behavior, concept formation, and school desegregation. A previous book, *The Human Subject in the Psychological Laboratory* (New York: Pergamon, 1977) is a critical examination of research philosophies and methodologies in the behavioral sciences.